DesigningBorders
forSunandShade

By Bob Hyland

Janet Marinelli
SERIES EDITOR

Sigrun Wolff Saphire
SENIOR EDITOR

Mark Tebbitt
SCIENCE EDITOR

Leah Kalotay
ART DIRECTOR

Joni Blackburn
COPY EDITOR

Steven Clemants
VICE-PRESIDENT,
SCIENCE &
PUBLICATIONS

Scot Medbury
PRESIDENT

Elizabeth Scholtz
DIRECTOR
EMERITUS

Handbook #183

Copyright © 2006 by Brooklyn Botanic Garden, Inc.

All-Region Guides, formerly *21st-Century Gardening Series,* are published three times a year at 1000 Washington Ave., Brooklyn, NY 11225.

Subscription included in Brooklyn Botanic Garden subscriber membership dues ($35 per year; $45 outside the United States).

ISBN-13: 978-1-889538-71-6
ISBN-10: 1-889538-71-X.

Printed by Science Press, a division of Cadmus Communications. Printed on recycled paper.

Cover: The entry garden at San Francisco Botanical Garden.
Above: Gorgeous to look at, this exuberant Pennsylvania garden is planted with a plethora of shrubs and perennials that offer permanent structure to the border as well as welcome habitat for local wildlife.

Designing Borders for Sun and Shade

Dazzling Borders for Sun and Shade

The art and practice of creating dynamic, colorful, four-season borders planted with a mixture of perennials, shrubs, ornamental grasses, annuals, and bulbs has come of age in America. I credit much of this development to the perennial-plants craze that has swept the country over the past two decades. Every year, choice sun- and shade-loving perennials are being introduced, and other groups of plants have been propelled into the limelight along with them. Plant hunters and breeders continue to expand and diversify the palette of exceptional flowering and foliage shrubs, grasses, and long-blooming annuals. Many are brand-new hybrids and cultivars; others are time-tested plants riding new waves of popularity. Never before has there been such a wealth and diversity of ornamental plants to combine in mixed borders.

Mixed borders have a more natural look than strictly homogeneous herbaceous borders. The well-designed mixed border is layered with plantings of ephemeral bulbs, grasses, ferns, and long-blooming annuals with perennials and shrubs the way nature does in the wild. Spring-blooming bulbs provide early-season color and are great companions with shrubs; then they leave the scene for other plants to shine. Annual flowers can fill gaps, offer quick color fixes, and play with the big guys—those glamorous perennials! Summer bulbs, tropicals, accent plants in pots, and even garden art add still more levels of interest.

A well-planned herbaceous perennial border offers interesting foliage, flowers, and seed heads for a long season. But a crucial design element is missing—permanency.

Backlit by the sun, the brilliant colors of *Canna* 'Pretoria' and Tropicana sizzle. Hot colors such as these are most effective where they can be viewed at close range.

Under a canopy of large trees and shrubs, lady slipper orchids and blue phlox put on a spring show in a northeastern woodland border.

Herbaceous borders lack woody evergreen or deciduous small trees and shrubs to contribute form, mass, texture, and color throughout the year—particularly winter. Conversely, mixed borders are melting pots for great plants of all kinds, generating excitement and exuberance year-round. They are also biologically diverse and create habitat niches for a variety of wildlife.

Don't get me wrong—American gardeners' love affair with perennials is still passionate. But not everyone wants to plant and maintain a "pure" perennial border, particularly in the grand English tradition, with its regimented masses of herbaceous plants in carefully orchestrated color sweeps and repeating patterns. We have long attempted to replicate this flower-heavy herbaceous-border style in North America using the same plants that thrive in England, and we've learned that it is not an easy task. Climate types and growing conditions in most regions of North America are very different from those of the British Isles. In many areas, summers are much hotter and more humid and the winters colder; other regions experience periodic drought or cycles of wet and dry weather.

Mixed Borders American-Style

North American gardeners are increasingly discovering and defining new mixed border styles based on regional climate and growing conditions. We are also becoming more ecologically aware, learning that not all plants grow well everywhere, and that while garden styles may reflect personal taste and choice, they are not always environmentally appropriate for all regions.

Mixed borders here in North America have evolved from a cross between the English flower border and shrubbery planted to ring and anchor the suburban house.

The flowers are a nice touch, but it's the distinctive textures and forms that make this California garden shine.

Evergreen and deciduous foundation shrubs, long-lived and offering reliable green substance and seasonal flowers, have long been accessorized with spots and splashes of perennials, annuals, and bulbs. But these compositions remained rather uninspired and predictable until the team of James van Sweden and Wolfgang Oehme introduced us to a new landscape style during the 1980s. Their approach capitalized on the growing interest in perennial plants and incorporated bold sweeps and masses of perennials and ornamental grasses with shrubs and trees in a more naturalistic style. At about the same time, California-based Rosalind Creasy threw out the rulebook on vegetable gardening and challenged us to look at the ornamental attributes of edibles like vegetables, fruits, and herbs. She demonstrated that they didn't have to be grown behind a fence in a segregated patch but could beautifully integrate with shrub-and-flower-border designs.

European landscape designers, particularly from Germany and Holland, have also influenced contemporary mixed border design. Dutch nurserymen and garden designers Piet Oudolf and Henk Gerritsen are broadening our vision of the mixed border by creating ethereal and lyrical moods and eliciting emotional responses through the deft use of plants. Employing plants with distinctive texture and form, a more natural appearance, and a subtle color palette, they are promoting a new naturalism for mixed borders.

Whether you're creating a landscape in the grassland or woodland regions of the Midwest, East, or Northwest or are an arid-climate gardener in Southern California or New Mexico, these exciting new trends in mixed border design will help you create a garden that is beautiful, regionally appropriate, and easier to maintain than the typical herbaceous-only planting.

Ten Steps to Designing a Border

Great mixed borders don't just happen. They start with dreams and visions that are brought to fruition with careful planning, planting, and garden maintenance. My border inspirations come from many sources—visits to fabulous public and private gardens, tantalizing pictures in glossy garden magazines, my work experiences at great botanical gardens across the country, and my own creative instincts. Whatever your inspiration, allow yourself the luxury and freedom to explore and dream a bit before developing a mixed border plan on paper.

Step 1: Locate the Border

Begin with the selection of a site. Choose a location suited to the overall layout of your property. Think in practical as well as aesthetic terms: Where is the water spigot? How far do you want to push a wheelbarrow or carry garden tools? Consider views from the house and outdoor living spaces like patios, decks, and terraces. Will the border be delineated by a wall of your house, living hedge, stone wall, fence, or the edge of a woodland?

Step 2: Assess Growing Conditions

Stand back and observe your prospective border location at different times of the day and from various perspectives. Study the movement of the sun and light patterns

Poking through tall upright gladioli, the wavy stems of catmint weave through the planting, adding depth to the border's mellow color scheme of white and purple.

across the site. How many hours of sun will the border receive in the course of the day? Will it be a sunny, partial-shade, or full-shade border? Will it get softer morning light or hot, glaring afternoon sun? If it is backlit by the sun, consider using ornamental grasses and perennials with silvery-green, chartreuse, and golden-variegated foliage for the most dramatic effect. Also think about when you will spend the most time viewing and enjoying your border.

Gauge the location's exposure to wind and consider how it will affect the design. Is the border sheltered and enclosed? Does it have a background hedge that acts as a windscreen? Or is it floating out in the open, with no buffer against the elements? Plants with delicate stems or top-heavy flower heads may require more staking in windy, exposed borders; some shrubs and grasses like pieris and fountain bamboo (*Fargesia nitida*) do not like cold, desiccating winter winds.

Now is a good time to take a soil sample from your proposed site and have it analyzed and do a percolation test to determine whether the soil drains freely or holds water. Your local county cooperative extension agent can help with these tests. Once you know the properties of the soil in your garden, you can better match plants to the site. The most regionally appropriate designs favor plants that thrive solely with natural rainfall. But if supplemental irrigation is required, you need to consider how you will deliver it to the border. I recommend a water-conserving drip-irrigation system designed to deliver water slowly in measured, small amounts to the root zone of plants. It can be as simple as a few soaker hoses made from recycled tires winding through the bed or a more elaborate system of tubing and emitters hidden underneath a layer of mulch. Plan for irrigation at the same time you develop your planting scheme to get an idea of the materials needed and the cost involved. However, I advise waiting to install soaker hoses and drip lines until after the initial planting to avoid slicing hoses when digging; you'll also want to direct water exactly where it is needed in newly planted beds.

Step 3: Determine Size and Shape

Carefully consider the best size and shape for your mixed border. Will it be a square or rectangle, or will it be a curving and sinuous form? Let existing features, such as the shape of the lawn or the building against which you plan to install the border, guide your design. If you have never delineated an outdoor garden space, I recommend staking the proposed corners with wood or bamboo stakes. Then run garden twine from stake to stake to outline the bed. For curvilinear designs, arrange a supple garden hose

To stand up to its imposing backdrop, this South Carolina border features large, bold plants that beautifully complement the color of the brickwork.

on the ground to approximate the design. Once you have an outline laid out, it is a cinch to move around the hose or stakes and string to make adjustments.

Don't skimp on the size of your border, but don't take on more than you can handle. You need ample space to accommodate a variety of plants for four seasons of interest, particularly for woody shrubs. Plan for 30 to 45 herbaceous plants and 3 to 5 woody shrubs at a minimum. And remember, the farther your garden is from your viewing point, the larger it must be to make a visual impact.

Consider access to the border as you develop your plan. You need to be able to reach all areas of the border from the edges or internal paths. By definition, mixed borders incorporate woody shrubs, which require space. Ideally a depth of 10 to 12 feet gives you the most flexibility. Since a person of average height can reach only about 2½ to 3 feet into a bed, a border that accommodates shrubs will probably need a central path, plus a rear one if the border is accessible from the front side only.

Step 4: Select a Style

Contemporary mixed border designs are strongly influenced by regional climate, vegetation types, soils, and other growing conditions. In the East and Northwest, where deciduous and coniferous forests prevail, you can use the woodland edge (where

The varied planting scheme of this meadow border carries through into fall when the drying stalks of feather reed grass and little bluestem join the fading foliage of willow-leafed amsonia and the dry seed heads of sedum and black-eyed Susans for a muted late-season display.

you've stopped mowing) as a backdrop or leafy, shade-dappled canopy for a mixed border. The "edge" may already have a shrubby layer of spicebush (*Lindera benzoin*), dogwoods (*Cornus*), birches (*Betula*), redbuds (*Cercis*), pieris, mountain laurel (*Kalmia latifolia*), cedars (*Juniperus* or *Thuja*), or Douglas fir (*Pseudotsuga menziesii*). You can integrate perennials like cranesbills (*Geranium*), coral bells (*Heuchera*), foam-flowers (*Tiarella*), meadow rues (*Thalictrum*), rodgersias, and bulbs like snowdrops (*Galanthus*) and summer snowflakes (*Leucojum aestivum*) for a "woodland" border look. You might also mark the transition to a sunnier area with shrub roses, hydrangeas, angelicas, colewort (*Crambe cordifolia*), perennial phlox, and big and little bluestems (*Andropogon* and *Schizachyrium*).

In dry desert and Mediterranean climates, great architectural effects can be achieved using the spiky, sword-shaped foliage of agaves, yuccas, cordylines, and New Zealand flaxes (*Phormium*), softened with cassias (*Senna*), lavenders, rockroses (*Cistus*), euphorbias, diascias, bulbines, bulbinellas, gladioli, salvias, and billowing grasses like Mexican feather grass (*Stipa tenuissima*).

Lush tropical mixed borders are appropriate and easy to grow in frost-free south Florida and Hawaii, where balmy temperatures and humidity are the norm. Gigantic, broad-leafed taro (*Colocasia esculenta*), bananas (*Musa*), palms, cannas, castor bean (*Ricinus communis*), and rice-paper plant (*Tetrapanax papyrifer*) command attention when artfully combined with the kaleidoscopic flower and leaf colors of coleus (*Solenostemon scutellarioides*), euphorbias, dahlias, flowering tobaccos (*Nicotiana*), hibiscus, gardenias, angel's trumpets (*Brugmansia*), and calla lilies (*Zantedeschia*). Through the Gulf Coast states and cool-temperate regions, many of these same plants will thrive during hot, humid summers but will be knocked back by frosts. Where winters are cold and the ground freezes for extended periods, most tropical plants are treated as annuals or are dug and stored indoors until the following growing season.

A naturalistic meadow or prairie style can be achieved by combining native ornamental grasses like switch grass (*Panicum virgatum*) and big and little bluestems (*Andropogon* and *Schizachyrium*) with shrubby sumacs (*Rhus*), dogwoods (*Cornus*), and ninebark (*Physocarpus opulifolius*), mixed with meadow composites like coneflowers (*Rudbeckia* and *Echinacea*), goldenrods (*Solidago*), ironweeds (*Vernonia*), and cup plants (*Silphium perfoliatum*) or compass plants (*S. laciniatum*).

My signature border style is a hybrid blend of regional styles combining strong yellows, oranges, and reds, architectural foliage, and ornamental grasses. It's a blousy, naturalistic, meadowlike style with a hint of the tropics that includes plants like cutleaf staghorn sumac (*Rhus typhina* 'Laciniata'), coralbark willow (*Salix alba* var. *vitellina* 'Britzensis'), red-osier dogwood (*Cornus sericea*), and chokeberries (*Aronia*) mixed with grasses like Korean feather reed grass (*Calamagrostis brachytricha*), switch grasses like *Panicum virgatum* 'Shenandoah' and 'Dallas Blues', great coneflowers (*Rudbeckia maxima*), and giant tickseed (*Coreopsis tripteris*). Ornamental onions (*Allium*), Tropicana and 'Pretoria' cannas, cockscombs like *Celosia* 'Flamingo Purple', and marigolds such as *Tagetes* 'Cinnabar' might lend annual seasonal color.

Step 5: Choose a Color Palette

One of the most important aspects of designing a mixed border is how plants are placed with regard to the color of their flowers and foliage. You can create peaceful, calming harmonies with subtle pastels or excite and jolt the viewer with contrasts of brilliant colors.

I advocate starting a border design by building upon a monochromatic color scheme. Do you like warm or hot colors like yellows, golds, oranges, and reds? Or do

your preferences lie with calming, less frenetic pinks, blues, and whites? Choose your favorite color and work from that starting point. It's not that different from selecting a wall paint color for a room in your home around which you add furnishings and fabrics, or selecting an outfit and accessories to wear to work.

Using gradations of one color makes it possible to focus on foliage and flower shapes and on the rhythm and structure of the planting. You can also create dramatic tension, increase perception, and manipulate mood. A border of yellow gives a sense of enlightenment and happiness. A border of blues and greens is more subtle, withdrawn and calming, while a composition of reds, violets, and oranges excites and energizes.

Color often dictates where and how plants are best placed in the border. Saturated reds and scarlets scream at you for attention. But since these hot colors are not deciphered at a distance, they are best placed closer to the viewer for full effect. Foliage plays an important color role too. A strong, metallic-bronze or deep burgundy leaf will give a sobering quality to a planting compared with green or yellow. The gray-greens of lavenders, artemisias, cheddar pinks (*Dianthus gratianopolitanus*), or lamb's ears (*Stachys byzantina*) teamed with pastel shades have a Mediterranean effect. Whites, silvers, and chartreuses in solids and variegated patterns help brighten up and enliven shady borders. If not used carefully, though, they can poke holes in compositions of mixed colors.

Step 6: Draw a Plan

Taking the time to make a plan or a quick, crude sketch of your border will pay off in the end. You don't need the drafting skills of a landscape architect or graphic artist to do this. A few simple tools are all you need to get started: a tape measure, a ruler or straightedge, plain or graph paper (the back of an envelope has also served me well for a quick sketch), and a pencil. The first step is to measure the actual dimensions of your prospective border (see step 3, above), along with other elements like buildings, paths, existing trees or hedges, and walls. Next it's to the drawing board. Decide on the scale for your drawing—a common scale is one square on the graph paper to two or three square feet of garden space. Tape a large sheet of graph paper to a flat table surface. Record on the paper the corners of the house, property lines, and other

continues on page 22

With a monochromatic color scheme such as this design of soft pinks, focus shifts from flower color to foliage and flower shapes. A few lively maroon accents add structure and variety to the border.

HOW TO BUILD A BORDER
Plant Selection Made Simple

The series of drawings that starts on the facing page and continues on pages 18 and 20 depicts the three major phases in the development of a 6- by 12-foot section of a mixed border planting. The first step is choosing the major anchor plants, such as shrubs and a background hedge, if appropriate. In the second phase, the herbaceous perennials that will provide most of the flower and foliage color and texture are selected. Phase three adds the icing to the cake: Bulbs and annuals are added to the mix to lengthen the season and offer nonstop color.

Phase One: Choosing Hedges and Shrubs

A hedge of upright yew (*Taxus × media* 'Hicksii') provides a dense, fine-needled evergreen background. It has been clipped here into a rather flat wall that defines the space, frames the border, and delineates boundaries. A deciduous hydrangea (*Hydrangea paniculata* Pink Diamond) is planted in front of the hedge, its coarse foliage set off by the finer-textured background hedge. In early spring before other perennials, grasses, and bulbs make their appearance, the hydrangea's sparse, naked branches are traced against the dark green of the yew. In summer, its long-lasting flowers open creamy white and become deep pink with a red reverse, adding further interest and texture to the shrub layer.

Shrubs Featured in This Planting

 1 *Hydrangea paniculata* Pink Diamond
 2 *Taxus × media* 'Hicksii'

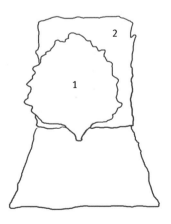

See the encyclopedia beginning on page 28 to choose plants appropriate to your climate and garden.

Phase Two: Choosing Perennials

Herbaceous perennials and spring bulbs are planted to fill in the scene. Just in front of the hydrangea, an eye-catching clump of perennial phlox (*Phlox paniculata* 'Düsterlohe', syn. 'Nicky') provides attractive straight vertical stems, clean foliage, and, in season, deeply saturated magenta blooms. A silvery-white variegated feather reed grass (*Calamagrostis* × *acutiflora* 'Avalanche') punctuates the border with airy flower stems that bridge the gap in height between the shrubby hydrangea and the much shorter phlox. A cluster of ornamental onions (*Allium aflatunense*) draw the eye to the middle of the border with a knockout display of four-inch globes of purplish-pink star-shaped flowers. Anchoring the front of the border is a softly mounded clump of spurge (*Euphorbia dulcis* 'Chameleon'). Its small greenish-yellow flowers are accented brilliantly against the rich purple foliage, which also picks up the flower shades of the phlox and ornamental onions. The spreading, arching red stems and green leaves of a low-growing succulent stonecrop (*Sedum* 'Ruby Glow') reiterates the overall color scheme, echoes the foliage texture of the spurge's succulent leaves, and connects the border planting to the ground.

Perennials Featured in This Planting

1 *Calamagrostis* × *acutiflora* 'Avalanche'
2 *Euphorbia dulcis* 'Chameleon'
3 *Phlox paniculata* 'Düsterlohe' (syn. 'Nicky')
4 *Sedum* 'Ruby Glow'

Spring Bulb

5 *Allium aflatunense*

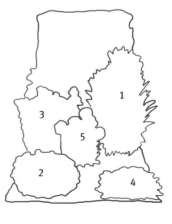

See the encyclopedia beginning on page 28 to choose plants appropriate to your climate and garden.

Phase Three: Choosing Annuals and Bulbs

By summer, the border is a symphony of pink, cerise, and burgundy tones backed by multitextured hues of green. Growing quickly with warm air and soil temperatures and long day length, summer-flowering annuals and summer bulbs weave together the mixed border. Vibrant *Crocosmia × crocosmiiflora* 'Emily McKenzie' erupts in mid-border, taking the place of the ornamental onions, which have by now faded. The crocosmia's branched spikes of bright orange flowers with mahogany throats provide contrast to the prevailing pink, purple, and magenta palette and blend nicely with the tawny vertical stems of the ripening feather reed grass, whose spires are echoed by its grassy foliage. With nodding flowers that begin white, age to pale pink, and finally fade to rose pink, annual flowering tobacco (*Nicotiana mutabilis*) provides a soft transition between the imposing shock of grass behind it and the rounded mound of stonecrop in front. As a bonus, it attracts hummingbirds to the scene. Bright pink-flowered *Petunia integrifolia* creeps along the front edge of the border and among the other plants, knitting all its bedfellows into a pleasing composition.

Annuals and Summer Bulbs Featured in This Planting

1 *Crocosmia × crocosmiiflora* 'Emily McKenzie'
2 *Nicotiana mutabilis*
3 *Petunia integrifolia*

See the encyclopedia beginning on page 28 to choose plants appropriate to your climate and garden.

continued from page 15

existing features that will act as reference points. Then spread a piece of tracing paper over your base map, sketch the shape and size of your future border on the tracing paper, and work on it until you like what you see.

When you are ready to select plants—my favorite part of mixed border design and likely yours, too—start by reading the plant descriptions in the "Encyclopedia of Plants for Sun and Shade" (page 28), keeping in mind light, soil, and moisture requirements. Make a list of appealing plants, noting flower color, bloom time, and dimensions of every plant. Once completed, your wish list will be useful throughout the design process.

Draw rough circles on your plan to indicate good places for single specimens or groupings of plants. I find it useful to cut pictures from magazines and plant catalogs to tape or glue to the plan to remind me of form and color.

Step 7: Decide on a Background

If your border design calls for creating a background hedge, decide if it will be evergreen or deciduous and site it on your plan first. Will it be clipped or sheared into a flat plane or allowed to grow naturally? Determine to what height you want the hedge to grow and how often it will require pruning. Six to eight feet is a good height for most background hedges. Some evergreen possibilities are yews (*Taxus*), junipers, northern white cedar, also known as eastern arborvitae (*Thuja occidentalis*), western red cedar (*Thuja plicata*), hollies (*Ilex*), myrtles (*Myrtus communis*), and photinias. A few deciduous choices are Amur privet (*Ligustrum amurense*), California privet (*L. ovalifolium*), European hornbeam (*Carpinus betulus*), and American beech (*Fagus grandifolia*).

Remember, the background for a mixed border does not necessarily have to be a formal hedge—it can simply borrow and capitalize on a woodland edge, the wall of your home, or even a stacked woodpile.

Step 8: Choose a Few Anchor Plants

After you decide on a background, the next step is to choose a few outstanding anchor shrubs. Consider bloom time, fruit color, and foliage texture in different seasons to strategically place them in your border. Remember how important shrubs are to the internal framework and four-season interest in the mixed border. In winter, shrubby deciduous dogwoods (*Cornus*) and willows (*Salix*) can add vibrant-colored stems; viburnums, beautyberries (*Callicarpa*), hollies (*Ilex*), and Oregon grape

Strategically placed, shrubs like the chartreuse-leafed *Sambucus* help to anchor the border and give it depth.

(*Mahonia aquifolium*) contribute colorful fruit; and Hinoki false cypress (*Chamaecyparis obtusa*), junipers, cedars (*Thuja*), and pieris lend evergreen foliage and texture to an otherwise barren, snow-covered border. In early spring the naked branches of deciduous shrubs frame early bulbs and emerging perennials. Many shrubs bloom throughout spring, but don't forget those that flower in summer like hydrangeas, hibiscus, smoke-bushes (*Cotinus*), roses, and old-fashioned weigelas. In autumn, shrubs like purple beautyberry (*Callicarpa dichotoma*), winterberry holly (*Ilex verticillata*), and *Hydrangea paniculata* provide foliage, fruit, and fading flower heads to the accompaniment of fall-blooming asters, Japanese anemones, coral bells (*Heuchera*), and toad lilies (*Tricyrtis*).

Once placed on your plan, shrubs become the foundations for focused plant combinations. To simplify the process of filling in with companion plantings, break the border into small vignettes of shrubs, perennials, ornamental grasses, annuals, and bulbs.

Step 9: Divide the Border into Small Vignettes

Start by picking perennials that bloom at the same time as the anchor shrubs or ones that complement their foliage colors and textures. A classic combination consists of lavenders, hyssops (*Agastache*), or catmints (*Nepeta*) with roses. To this mix add feathery silver-gray *Artemisia* 'Powis Castle' or large woolly lambs' ears like *Stachys* 'Helene von Stein'.

Don't place too many similar shapes or plants of the same height together, as this breeds monotony. With too much sameness, your border may appear flat and lack rhythm. For contrast, place softer, rounded forms such as spurge (*Euphorbia dulcis*), catmint (*Nepeta faassenii*), and 'Bowles' Mauve' wallflower (*Erysimum* 'Bowles'

For four-season interest, choose a few shrubs like American cranberry bush that counter the bleakness of winter with displays of brightly colored fruit.

Mauve') next to stiff, spiky plants like *Yucca filamentosa,* red-hot poker (*Kniphofia uvaria*), and New Zealand flax (*Phormium tenax*). A general rule that is often promoted for border designs is shorter plants (one foot high or less) along the edges, medium-height plants (two to four feet) in the middle, and taller specimens (five to seven feet) in the back of the border. But I feel that mixed borders should not be so staged and contrived but rather should have a more natural look. So don't follow this rule too closely. Position and allow taller perennials to erupt through and punctuate shorter plant groupings in the middle, corners, or other strategic locations in the border. You can achieve wonderful effects with see-through plants like meadow rues (*Thalictrum*), Russian sage (*Perovskia atriplicifolia*), or purple moor grass (*Molinia caerulea*), which reach new heights when in bloom but nevertheless allow glimpses of neighboring plants thanks to their wiry and transparent flower stems.

Choose plants for season-long interest in your border. The secret to successful design lies in understanding how plants change and evolve through the growing season and applying this knowledge to combine them for continuous interest. You can interplant perennials, grasses, and bulbs so that combinations of spring bloomers are upstaged in summer by new combinations of flowers that are in turn succeeded by fall bloomers. In a shady border composition, Japanese kerria (*Kerria japonica*), green-and-gold (*Chrysogonum virginianum*), and narcissus can seamlessly flow into cranesbills (*Geranium*) and coral bells (*Heuchera*) in the same area. As this display passes its peak, a vignette of hydrangeas, hostas, bugbanes (*Actaea*), sedges (*Carex*), and fall crocuses captures your attention elsewhere in the border. In the sun, a

grouping of early-spring-flowering witch hazels (*Hamamelis × intermedia*) and crocuses (*Crocus* and *Colchicum*) fade from bloom to be succeeded in the border by
patches of ornamental onions (*Allium*), columbines (*Aquilegia*), catmints (*Nepeta*),
and cheddar pinks (*Dianthus gratianopolitanus*). This grouping is followed in another part of the border by oriental poppies (*Papaver orientale*), yarrows (*Achillea*),
phlox, and ornamental oreganos. A finale of bluebeard (*Caryopteris × clandonensis*),
ornamental grasses, asters, and salvias rides out the growing season. There are always
expected, as well as unexpected, opportunities. When you know that a plant like oriental poppy goes dormant in summer after bloom, you can plan for annual flowers
like flowering tobaccos (*Nicotiana*) and summer bulbs like *Gladiolus callianthus* to
fill the vacant space.

Step 10: Choose Plants Linking the Vignettes

Once you have orchestrated these smaller plant compositions, it is time to meld the
vignettes together into a cohesive design, keeping an eye on the whole. Take advantage of soft, spilling, and airy plants like catmints (*Nepeta*), lavenders, euphorbias,
ornamental onions (*Allium*), oreganos, and sprawling plants such as winecups
(*Callirhoe involucrata*), verbenas (*Verbena bipinnatifida, V. peruviana*), fleeceflowers
such as *Polygonum* 'Red Dragon' or cranesbills like *Geranium* 'Dilys' and Rozanne to
weave together plant compositions and unify the border design. Keep linking pleasing, varied plant combinations until you have filled your border. Be sure to repeat a
key plant, color, or strong form throughout the border to maintain unity and create
rhythm. In my border designs, the repetition of plants like the catmints *Nepeta ×
faassenii* 'Walker's Low' or 'Six Hill's Giant' and the feather reed grass *Calamagrostis
× acutiflora* 'Karl Foerster' act as common threads to tie everything together.

Once you have your first draft of a planting plan, tuck it into a drawer and review
it a few days later. With a fresh perspective you'll no doubt make some changes, but
don't get carried away with multiple revisions on paper and in your head—finessing
your design really happens on site when you are planting.

Finishing Touches

Mixed borders, like most garden designs, take two to three seasons to mature and fill
in. In the early stages, before the border has seamlessly knit together, I like to strategically position art objects like terra-cotta pots filled with statuesque plants, glazed
urns filled with water, and the occasional gazing ball.

Giving the design rhythm and helping the eye move along the border, mounds of *Hakonechloa macra* 'Aureola' bracket small groupings of blue-flowering plants.

Garden ornaments can also add charm to an established mixed border. Where vertical relief is needed, incorporating a rustic tepee covered with annual morning glories or a classic cone-shaped *tuteur* for rambling roses, clematis, or other vines may be a good option. I am fond of found objects with a sense of place. I inherited an assortment of bocce and lawn-bowling balls with our current property and like to dot them in my mixed borders to add an element of surprise and to echo flower colors. They are known to migrate about the border (as does a small flock of pink flamingoes) during the season for a touch of whimsy and amusement. Be adventurous. If something doesn't work or simply looks silly or out of place, you can always move it.

As your border matures, some plants will die and others will prove to be vigorous garden thugs and engulf their neighbors. Mistakes you may have made will become apparent. View these defects as opportunities to fine-tune your design. Watch how the composition develops and observe the changes that nature makes to improve on your ideas. It's always a pleasure to try new plants and combinations. A mixed border is never finished.

Design Tips

Here are some broad-brush principles that I use when creating a mixed border. Look at them as general guidelines, and don't get bogged down in design theory. Let your own creativity flow freely and express itself.

Right plant, right place! Use plants that like the growing conditions in your garden. Examine sun and shade patterns as well as the soil's composition, moisture, and pH, then focus on plants that thrive in those conditions.

Be environmentally in tune. Consider plants that are native or well adapted to your region and that don't require lots of intervention or extraordinary energy to grow. Look to local plant communities for cues and models on how to structure your border design. Consider the regional characteristics of your border site: Is it woodland edge, chaparral hillside, rocky slope, open prairie, marsh, desert basin, or rainforest? The overall appearance of local natural areas and common plant traits can help steer your choices and define "the look" of your mixed border. Many plants that are native to your region make wonderful garden plants, and oftentimes cultivated varieties and forms have been selected or bred to increase the diversity of flower, foliage, and fruit colors and forms.

Capitalize on seasonality. By design, mixed borders should ride the four seasons with exceptional color, foliage, fruits, and structure, whether you garden in the warmer regions of the Deep South or in the coldest northern climates.

Avoid a hodgepodge of one-of-a-kind plants. Group plants in multiples of threes, fives, and sevens (a prime element of Zen gardens that works well in mixed borders too).

Balance spontaneity and control. Create moments of harmony and tension in your design with colors, textures, shapes, and sizes. One method is to let most plants grow in their natural forms while pruning or shearing a few to create contrast.

Choreograph movement and rhythm. Choose plants that dance in the wind or hum and reverberate with pollinators like birds, bees, and butterflies. The placement of plant groups in repeating colors and forms can also create visual rhythm. To move the viewer's eye through the border, I often repeat upright conifers and sheared evergreens, billowing grasses, red- or yellow-twigged dogwoods (*Cornus*), and color drifts of phlox, yarrows (*Achillea*), catmints (*Nepeta*), astilbes, euphorbias, and salvias.

Use light to advantage. Integrate plants whose flower color and foliage reflect or absorb sunlight to create depth, shadow play, and color intensity in the border from first morning to early evening.

Create focal points that capture the eye, ear, and nose. A beautiful, well-sited specimen shrub, yucca, or ornamental grass with strong form and structure can command initial attention and then lead the eye to other attractions. Dramatic foliage, a huge drift of color, plants that rustle and whisper in the wind, enticing fragrances, and man-made garden structures and ornaments also add points of focus in the border.

Encyclopedia of Plants for Sun and Shade

This plant encyclopedia is divided into two parts. On pages 30 to 78 you will find plants suitable for a sunny mixed border. On pages 79 to 110 are plants for a shady garden. Each section is subdivided into five categories: shrubs, perennials, grasses, annuals, and bulbs. Each entry in turn discusses several species and related cultivars and gives tips for growing the plants as well as how best to combine them with other plants. All plants featured in this encyclopedia have been carefully chosen to provide a wide range of forms, colors, and textures, and all have great dramatic presence. To find the plants that will thrive in your region, USDA hardiness zones are included for eastern gardeners and Sunset zones for western gardeners.

To avoid confusion about plant cultivar names rarely used in commerce, we have strayed from the strict rules of horticultural nomenclature by adopting the following two conventions. First, if a plant is more commonly known by its trade name than by its assigned cultivar name, we list it by its trade name, capitalized but without the single quotes normally used for cultivar names. For example, the rose selection 'Radrazz' is generally listed by U.S. plant suppliers as *Rosa* Knock Out, so the encyclopedia entry lists it as Knock Out. Second, when a direct English translation of an original non-English cultivar name is the most commonly known name, such as *Sedum* 'Autumn Joy' for *S.* 'Herbstfreude', the better-known name is used.

Mixed-border garden designs use shrubs, herbaceous perennials, grasses, annuals, and bulbs for a natural-looking blend of proportions and textures; a manmade birdhouse or other ornament highlights the effect.

Shrubs for Sun

Buxus | Boxwood

Boxwoods are useful for their dense evergreen foliage, curvaceous shape, and ability to withstand clipping. Most species are slow growing and the ideal size for mixed borders. The small, rounded to lance-shaped leaves offer a nice green sheen, but in cold-winter climates they may discolor to yellowish green or golden bronze.

Native Habitat Rocky hills to woodlands in Central America, West Indies, Europe, Africa, Korea, and Japan

Hardiness Zones USDA 5–9; Sunset 3–24, 26–34, 39

Growing Tips Full sun or partial shade. Loamy, well-drained soils. Ideal for topiary. Protect from winter winds.

Cultivars and Related Species *Buxus sempervirens* 'Suffruticosa' is compact and very slow growing to six feet tall;

Japanese boxwood (*B. microphylla* var. *japonica*) has glossier foliage and similar habit; Sheridan hybrids (*B. microphylla* var. *koreana* × *B. sempervirens*) 'Green Mountain' and 'Green Velvet' are compact forms with good dark green winter color and better cold hardiness (USDA 4–9; Sunset 2–24, 26–41).

Companion Plants Use boxwood as an evergreen backdrop or as sculpted punctuation points in borders. Combine it with pinks (*Dianthus*), dwarf asters, penstemons, and ornamental grasses with silvery-blue foliage, like blue oat grass (*Helictotrichon sempervirens*) and blue fescues (*Festuca*).

Callicarpa dichotoma | Purple Beautyberry

Purple beautyberry takes center stage in the border after autumn leaf drop, when eye-catching violet-purple fruit in bead-like clusters dot the upright stems. The rest of the season, this three- to four-foot shrub offers arching form, bright green leaves, and shy pale pink flower clusters in leaf axils.

Native Habitat Woodlands in China, Korea, Japan

Hardiness Zones USDA 5–8; Sunset 3–9, 14–24, 29–41

Growing Tips Full sun or dappled shade. Fertile, well-drained soils. In cold-climate regions, treat as a dieback shrub and cut stems to the ground in late winter to encourage new spring growth.

Cultivars and Related Species *Callicarpa dichotoma* 'Early Amethyst' has purple fruits that are quick to color in late summer; *C.* 'Profusion' offers violet fruits in copious clusters of 30 to 40; native

In addition to its striking fall fruit, purple beautyberry has a graceful, arching form to recommend it.

Bluebeard's gray-green foliage and long-lasting blooms add zest to the border in late summer.

American beautyberry (*C. americana*) is a coarse, eight- to ten-foot-tall shrub with violet-magenta fruits that is appropriate for large, informal borders.

Companion Plants Low-growing bugleweeds (*Ajuga*), spotted deadnettles such as *Lamium maculatum* 'Beacon Silver' and 'Shell Pink', black mondo grass *Ophiopogon* 'Nigrescens', and eastern bleeding heart (*Dicentra eximia*), make good bedfellows.

Caryopteris × *clandonensis* Bluebeard

Bluebeard is an unsurpassed shrub for its blue, late-summer flowers in both axillary and terminal clusters, which last for several weeks. This mounded shrub, which grows two to three feet high and wide, is covered with soft gray-green, aromatic foliage.

Native Habitat Garden hybrid

Hardiness Zones USDA 5–9; Sunset 3–7, 14–17, 29–41

Growing Tips Full sun and dry soils; thrives on neglect. Cut to the ground annually in late winter to promote vigorous growth for the coming season. Plants bloom on new wood and will flower by late summer.

Cultivars and Related Species *Caryopteris* × *clandonensis* 'Longwood Blue' bears silvery-gray leaves and violet-blue flowers; 'Dark Knight' offers deep blue-purple flowers; and 'Worcester Gold' is a standout for its yellow foliage and blue flowers.

Companion Plants As summer begins to wane, along comes bluebeard. It makes nice compositions with other aromatic herbs like rosemary (*Rosmarinus officinalis*), salvias, and lavender cotton (*Santolina chamaecyparissus*) as well as late-blooming daylilies such as *Hemerocallis* 'Autumn Minaret' and autumn bulbs like *Colchicum autumnale*, *Sternbergia lutea*, or *Crocus sativus*.

Chamaecyparis obtusa 'Nana Gracilis' | 'Nana Gracilis' Hinoki False Cypress

This Hinoki false cypress cultivar is an aristocratic dwarf evergreen well suited for mixed borders. It grows slowly into a pyramidal shape six to eight feet high without pruning and shaping. Flattened sprays of dark green foliage give the shrub a soft, layered appearance.

Native Habitat Garden origin

Hardiness Zones USDA 5–8; Sunset 4–6, 15–17, 32–34

Growing Tips Full sun to partial shade. Well-drained neutral to slightly acid soils. Tolerates heat and drought.

A standard-size false cypress can provide vertical interest in spacious gardens (left), but dwarf cultivars are often more suitable for mixed borders. The bark of red-osier dogwood, such as the yellow-twigged 'Silver and Gold' (right), adds brightness to the border from autumn deep into the winter.

Cultivars and Related Species A flat-topped dwarf to six feet tall, *Chamaecyparis obtusa* 'Nana Aurea' has rich golden-yellow foliage; *C. pisifera* 'Filifera Aurea,' a Sawara cypress cultivar, grows into a pyramidal haystack form with unusual stringy, golden-yellow foliage.

Companion Plants Dwarf Hinoki false cypress calls for refined, flowing plants as neighbors. Ornamental grasses such as Hakone grasses (*Hakonechloa*), palm sedge (*Carex muskingumensis*), and the golden wood millet *Milium effusum* 'Aureum' offer contrast and rhythm. Native Allegheny spurge (*Pachysandra procumbens*), dwarf goatsbeard (*Aruncus aethusifolius*), and coral bells (*Heuchera*) are also good companions.

Cornus sericea (syn. C. stolonifera) Red-Osier Dogwood

This shrubby, green-leafed native dogwood grabs the stage in the winter border with its bright red stems. Flat-topped white flower clusters appear in summer followed by short-lived white fruits. Cultivars provide variegated leaves with artful patterns of chartreuse, golden yellow, and silvery white.

Native Habitat Wet, swampy areas in eastern North America

Hardiness Zones USDA 2–8; Sunset 1–9, 14–21, 31–45

Growing Tips Full sun to partial shade. Highly adaptable to a wide range of soil types. Thrives in moist locations. For maximum stem color, prune out a third of the oldest canes or cut to the ground in late winter.

Cultivars and Related Species *Cornus sericea* 'Cardinal' offers a striking bright cherry-red winter twig color; 'Silver and Gold' has golden-yellow winter stems and cream-edged leaves; the bloodtwig dogwood (*C. sanguinea*) cultivar 'Winter Flame' dazzles with a medley of yellow, orange, and pink tones.

Companion Plants Nestle red-osier dogwood near needled or broad-leafed evergreens like boxwoods (*Buxus*) or Hinoki false cypress (*Chamaecyparis obtusa*). Cultivars with variegated leaves make great companions with coneflowers (*Rudbeckia* and *Echinacea*) and pink and red salvias. The burgundy-leafed switch grass *Panicum virgatum* 'Shenandoah' echoes the red stem color.

Cotinus coggygria | Smoke Bush

Smoke bush is a great border shrub with the ability to completely transform its appearance and texture when in bloom. The common name is derived from the fading flowers—technically fuzzy hairs on stems of the multibranched inflorescence—which pass through several color changes during the season, at their best resembling dramatic puffs of pinkish smoke. Smoke bush is naturally multi-stemmed and creates a broad, spreading, ten-foot mass in borders. It often lends yellow to orange and red foliage color to the border in autumn.

Native Habitat Rocky sites in southern U.S. and from Mediterranean region to China

Hardiness Zones USDA 4–8; Sunset 2–4, 29–41

Growing Tips Full sun to partial shade (purple-leafed forms color best in full sun). Moderately fertile, moist but well-drained soils. Prune purple-leafed types to the ground in late winter to force vigorous shoot growth that is more vividly colored.

Cultivars and Related Species Of the purple-leafed types, *Cotinus coggygria* 'Royal Purple' sports the deepest, darkest red-purple foliage and turns scarlet in autumn; inflorescences have a purple haze. 'Daydream' offers a dense habit with green leaves and abundant fluffy brownish-pink inflorescences that persist longer than the species and other cultivars.

Companion Plants Site dark-foliaged smoke bush as a fuzzy backdrop to catmints (*Nepeta*), thread-leafed tickseed (*Coreopsis verticillata*), penstemons, and perennial phlox, as well as Russian sage (*Perovskia*), wormwood *Artemisia* 'Powis Castle', and lamb's ears (*Stachys byzantina*).

Hamamelis × *intermedia* Witch Hazel

Witch hazels ignite the late-winter mixed border. Spidery flowers unfurl on leafless stems in colors from yellow to orange, red, and reddish purple from midwinter through early spring. The coarse foliage has a nice green luster that

To extend the floral beauty of the mixed border across the seasons, include shrubs that offer early blooms, such as 'Jelena' witch hazel (left), as well as late-summer bloomers like 'Diana' rose of Sharon (right).

transforms to shades of autumn yellow, orange, and red. It has a generally upright-spreading, 10- to 15-foot, loosely branched habit.

Native Habitat Garden hybrid

Hardiness Zones USDA 5–8; Sunset 4–7, 15–17, 31–34, 39

Growing Tips Full sun to partial shade. Moist, acid, well-drained soils. Resents heavy pruning. Remove root suckers on grafted plants.

Cultivars and Related Species *Hamamelis × intermedia* 'Arnold Promise' offers clear yellow, fragrant flowers and a vase shape in the border; 'Jelena' sports fiery copper-orange flowers in great profusion; Chinese witch hazel (*H. mollis*) is notable for its intense fragrance, yellow flowers, and more compact habit.

Companion Plants Early-flowering spring bulbs like *Crocus tommasinianus* or *Scilla siberica* and lungworts (*Pulmonaria*) are good border mates. The fall foliage of billowing golden yellow to deep burgundy switch grasses (*Panicum virgatum*) offer nice color and textural contrast to coarse-leafed witch hazels.

Hibiscus syriacus | Rose of Sharon

Rose of Sharon illuminates the late-summer border with large, hollyhock-like flowers in long-lasting colors from white to red, purple, and violet. It is a real season-extending shrub with erect branches and bushy habit to eight feet tall. The dark green glossy leaves are three-lobed with toothed edges. Five-chambered brown capsules provide winter interest.

Native Habitat Moist woodlands in China and India

Hardiness Zones USDA 5–9; Sunset 2–21, 26, 28–41

Growing Tips Easy to grow. Full sun to partial shade. Moist, well-drained soils.

Cultivars and Related Species *Hibiscus syriacus* 'Diana' offers large, pure white flowers over a long period of time; 'Bluebird' is a favorite cultivar, with single lilac-blue flowers with a small red center. In hotter climates, Hawaiian hibiscus (*H. rosa-sinensis*) shouts with vibrant crimson, orange, yellow, or white flowers.

Companion Plants Hot plants with a tropical flair like hybrid cannas (such as *Canna* 'Australia') or bananas (*Musa*) cavort nicely. For a cooler effect, the steely foliage of blue oat grass (*Helictotrichon sempervirens*) or the glaucous leaves of *Rudbeckia maxima* are nice complements to *Hibiscus syriacus* 'Bluebird.'

Hydrangea | Hydrangea

Hydrangeas are the belles of the mixed border. Multiseason shrubs that lend dramatic flower, foliage, and winter interest, their big, snowball-like flower clusters may be white, pink, red, or blue and flat-topped, domed, or conical. The flower heads are composed of both tiny fertile flowers and larger sterile flowers with showy, petallike sepals. They are almost everlasting, transforming over the weeks from bright tones to papery brown. Some species offer bronzy-crimson fall leaf color.

Native Habitat Woodlands of North and South America and eastern Asia

Hardiness Zones USDA 4–9; Sunset 1–21, 14–24, 26, 28–43

Growing Tips Full sun to partial shade. Moist, organic, well-drained soils. Prune

Hydrangea flower heads can take many forms, from round to flat-topped, domed, or conical, like this oakleaf hydrangea cultivar, 'Snow Queen'.

after flowering, since flower buds are generally produced on previous year's wood.

Cultivars and Related Species So many hydrangeas—so little time! There are several outstanding cultivars of oakleaf hydrangea: *Hydrangea quercifolia* 'Snow Queen' offers deeply lobed, oaklike foliage and large cone-shaped flower clusters of pure white that shift to pinkish purple and then brown; a standard for the border is *H. arborescens* 'Annabelle', a smooth hydrangea that sports foot-wide globular clusters of sterile white flowers. Peegee hydrangea (*H. paniculata* 'Grandiflora') is a larger shrub that blooms in midsummer with conical flower heads of mostly sterile flowers; Pink Diamond is a newer introduction with white flower heads that fade to deep pink with a red reverse.

Companion Plants Hydrangeas are at home in the company of summer bloomers like rose of sharon (*Hibiscus syriacus*), *Rosa* 'Nearly Wild', thread-

leafed tickseed (*Coreopsis verticillata*), coral bells (*Heuchera*), and fall-blooming anemones (*Anemone* × *hybrida*).

Ilex | Holly

Hollies are often grown as a sheared hedge behind a mixed border or as small groupings or single specimens within the design. They provide exceptional evergreen foliage, often armed with prickly spines. Individually, many species grow too large for mixed borders. But there are several hollies, both evergreen and deciduous, that are of smaller scale. The flowers are usually inconspicuous, but they are very fragrant and attract bees. Perhaps holly's most striking contribution to a border design is the colorful fall and winter berries in red, black, yellow, and coral orange.

Native Habitat Woodlands in temperate regions

Hardiness Zones USDA 5–9; Sunset 2–24, 26, 28–43

Growing Tips Full sun or partial shade. Moderately fertile, moist but well-drained, humus-rich soil. Prune in late winter or early spring prior to flowering. Female plants require a nearby male pollinator for best fruit set.

Cultivars and Related Species *Ilex glabra* (inkberry), a North American native growing to ten feet, offers glossy green foliage and small black fruits; its Asian relative, Japanese holly (*I. crenata*), has lustrous dark green oval leaves that are turned under at the edges and shiny black fruit. There is nothing quite like the red fruit of winterberry holly (*I. verticillata*) contrasted against leafless, dark gray-black stems in the winter border; 'Winter Red' and 'Winter Gold' are desirable selections with heavy fruit set.

Companion Plants Hollies provide green background to flowering perennials and ornamental grasses in all seasons; I particularly like to partner them with coneflowers (*Rudbeckia* and *Echinacea*) and switch grasses (*Panicum*) that carry through fall and winter.

Physocarpus opulifolius | Ninebark

Ninebark is a native, thicket-forming shrub that grows to eight to ten feet tall. The species is rarely sought after, but a few cultivars are highly valued for their dark brown-purple or gold foliage. The leaves are generally three-lobed and toothed on the margins. In early summer, small, dense clusters of pink-tinged white flowers reveal themselves, followed by clusters of unique bladderlike red fruit. Older shrubs develop stringy, peeling bark of winter interest.

Used both as a hedge and specimen shrub, hollies, such as this winterberry holly, are especially valued for their bright-colored fall and winter fruit.

Many shrubs, such as Diabolo ninebark (left), are sought after for their unusual leaf color or variegation. Pittosporums (right) are also grown as border backdrops for their attractive leaf shape and evergreen foliage.

Native Habitat Thickets and rocky slopes in eastern North America

Hardiness Zones USDA 3–7; Sunset 1–3, 10, 32–45

Growing Tips Full sun. Moderately fertile, sharply drained soil. Prune out suckers in the border to keep in bounds.

Cultivars and Related Species *Physocarpus opulifolius* Diabolo offers lasting brownish-purple leaves that create an attractive dark backdrop for other border companions; 'Dart's Gold' is more compact, four to five feet tall, with golden-yellow foliage that fades in summer.

Companion Plants Play a fiery reddish-orange yarrow (*Achillea* 'Fireland'), a magenta phlox like *Phlox paniculata* 'Düsterlohe' ('Nicky'), prairie cone-flower (*Ratibida pinnata*), or a hot orange dahlia like 'Forncett Furnace' against the dark foliage of *Physocarpus*

opulifolius Diabolo. Contrast dark-leafed cannas 'Intrigue' or yellow-striped 'Striata' (syn. 'Pretoria') with *P. opulifolius* 'Dart's Gold'.

Pittosporum | Pittosporum
Pittosporums are valued for their attractive evergreen foliage—glossy yellowish-green to dark green leaves arranged simply or in whorls. These dependable border shrubs have creamy-white to yellow flowers borne singly in leaf axils or terminal umbel-like clusters. Depending on the species, the flowers can exude a very sweet, orange-blossom scent. The spherical woody capsules that follow add winter interest.

Native Habitat Grasslands to rainforests in Australia, New Zealand, China, Korea, and Japan

Hardiness Zones USDA 9–10; Sunset 8–31

Growing Tips Full sun or partial shade. Fertile, moist, well-drained soil. Variegated and purple-leafed selections retain best leaf color in full sun.

Cultivars and Related Species Japanese pittosporum (*Pittosporum tobira*) offers fragrant flowers and dense, lustrous deep green leaves with edges that curl under. Tawhiwhi (*P. tenuifolium*) is finer textured, and the leathery, mid-green leaves with wavy edges contrast nicely against dark gray to black stems; particularly nice selections include 'Nigricans', with blackish foliage, and 'Purpureum', with purplish leaves.

Companion Plants *Pittosporum* looks at home with New Zealand flax (*Phormium tenax*), cranesbills (*Geranium*), twinspurs (*Diascia*), and goatsbeards (*Aruncus*).

Rosa | Rose

Roses look great in the company of other shrubs, perennials, and annuals, rather than corralled in a rose garden. There are a multitude of heirloom shrub roses and modern landscape roses that offer beautiful flower color and form, long bloom, tantalizing fragrance, and colorful hips. Hybrid tea roses really shine in a mixed border, where neighboring plants can soften an awkward, rigid habit or hide less-than-perfect foliage. Climbers and ramblers can be trained along a wall or fence, adding texture and color.

Native Habitat Wide variety of habitats in North America, Europe, North Africa, and Asia

Hardiness Zones USDA 2–9; Sunset 1–24, 30–45

Growing Tips Full sun. Moderately fertile, moist but well-drained, humus-rich soil.

Cultivars and Related Species One of my favorite roses for the mixed border is *Rosa glauca* (syn. *R. rubrifolia*), which has grayish-purple foliage and small, single cerise-pink flowers with golden centers in late spring to early summer. Stunning orange-red hips follow and persist in fall and winter. *R. × odorata* 'Mutabilis' is another good performer for warmer climates, with pale pink double, two- to three-inch flowers, good form, light green leaves, and prickly stems. Winter-hardy and low-maintenance *R.* Carefree Beauty is an upright spreader bearing clusters of classic, semidouble mid-pink blooms continuously from spring to fall. Newcomer *R.* Knock Out sports fluorescent cherry-red blooms and exhibits disease resistance and continuous bloom at its best.

Companion Plants Roses combine nicely with lavenders, catmints (*Nepeta*), *Agastache* 'Blue Fortune', Russian sage (*Perovskia atriplicifolia*), and the large-leafed *Stachys* 'Helene von Stein', with its felty gray-green foliage.

Sambucus | Elderberry

The word is out that elderberries make fantastic border plants. They have compound, layered foliage and massive flat-topped heads of ivory white or pink flowers in late spring, followed by red, black, or white fruit clusters. Hybridizers have tinkered with the European species and come up with some beautiful golden-yellow, coppery-black, and variegated leaf forms.

Native Habitat Woodlands and thickets in temperate and subtropical regions of North and South America, Eurasia, Africa, and Australia

Hardiness Zones USDA 3–9; Sunset 1–7, 14–17 (vary by species)

Black-leafed elderberry cultivars provide brilliant contrast for light-colored plants in the mixed border.

Growing Tips Full sun or partial shade (some colored leaf forms are best in partial shade). Moist but well-drained, moderately fertile, humus-rich soil. Tolerates hard pruning in fall or spring to restrict size in the border.

Cultivars and Related Species American elder (*Sambucus nigra* subsp. *canadensis*) is stoloniferous and has upright, arching stems and purple-black fruit. Its close relative *S. racemosa* is bushier, with arching stems and red fruit; a cultivar, 'Sutherland Gold', has elegant deeply cut golden-yellow foliage and a very graceful habit. Black elderberry (*S. nigra* subsp. *nigra*) shows a more upright form and habit, with thick stems and glossy black fruit; Black Beauty offers intriguing dark black foliage and pink flowers in June.

Companion Plants Combine *Sambucus racemosa* 'Sutherland Gold' with the yellow-margined palm sedge *Carex muskingumensis* 'Oehme' or the black mondo grass *Ophiopogon* 'Nigrescens'. Accent *S. nigra* subsp. *nigra* Black Beauty with blue oat grass (*Helictotrichon sempervirens*) and *Rosa glauca*.

Senna (syn. *Cassia*) | Cassia, Senna

Cassias are outstanding foliage plants with compound leaves, bright golden-yellow pealike flowers, and persistent ornamental bean pods. Some species sport soft, silver-gray, finely divided leaves; others have large, tropical compound leaves up to 30 inches long.

Native Habitat Moist woodlands and scrub from eastern U.S., Brazil, Argentina, Australia, New Zealand, and Africa to Southeast Asia

Hardiness Zones USDA 4–11; Sunset 8–9, 12–16, 18–27

Growing Tips Average soils with good drainage. Prune after flowering. Some

Cassias have lacy, pealike foliage and flowers, and their attractive seedpods last into the winter.

species are frost tender and must be over-wintered indoors or treated as annuals.

Cultivars and Related Species *Senna artemisioides* with its silver, feathery foliage and yellow flowers is well accli-mated to interior desert regions of the Southwest and coastal California. Wild senna (*S. marilandica*) is a multi-stemmed herbaceous shrub with com-pound leaves and six-inch racemes of yellow flowers in mid- to late summer that is better suited to the midwestern and eastern U.S. (USDA 4–7; Sunset 1–10, 14, 28–43).

Companion Plants Use cassias for foliage effect and warm border color. Contrasting shrubs and perennials with reddish-purple foliage such as the smoke bush *Cotinus coggygria* 'Royal Robe', ninebark *Physocarpus opulifolius* Diabolo, or rose mallow *Hibiscus* 'Kopper King' make kinetic partners. Other good neighbors include yuccas or dark-leafed plants like *Canna* 'Intrigue', the castor bean *Ricinis communis* 'Carmencita', or the taro *Colocasia* 'Black Magic'.

Syringa meyeri | Meyer Lilac
Most cultivars of common lilac (*Syringa vulgaris*) grow too large for mixed bor-ders, but Meyer lilac, a compact, rounded shrub that grows four to eight feet tall, is a perfect fit. Small, oval leaves give it a fine texture, and it is a strong spring bloomer with small clusters of bluish or lavender-pink flowers that are reddish when in bud.

Native Habitat Woodlands and scrub of eastern Asia, particularly Korea

Hardiness Zones USDA 4–7; Sunset 1–9, 14–16, 32–43

Growing Tips Full sun. Fertile, humus-rich, neutral to alkaline, well-drained soils. Deadhead faded flower clusters before fruits form.

To keep lilacs from overwhelming the border, look for species and cultivars of compact size and mounding habit, such as *Syringa meyeri* or *S.* 'Miss Kim', above.

Cultivars and Related Species *Syringa* 'Miss Kim' forms a mounded plant to eight feet tall with coarse, leathery dark green foliage that turns a pleasing reddish purple in autumn. The purple flower buds open to icy-pink flowers.

Companion Plants Lilacs are good bedfellows with squills (*Scilla siberica*), catmints (*Nepeta*), Siberian iris (*Iris sibirica*), peonies, cranesbills (such as *Geranium phaeum* 'Samobor'), and ornamental onions like *Allium karataviense*.

Tibouchina urvilleana | Glory Bush

This shrub offers tantalizing foliage and satiny, saucer-shaped flowers of deep royal purple. Glory bush grows eight to ten feet tall, and its strongly veined, velvety, mid- to dark green leaves provide a rich, soft texture to the mixed border. New growth, branch tips, and buds are covered with reddish-orange hairs. In cooler climates, grow it in a container nestled in the border or enjoy it as an annual.

Native Habitat Rainforests of Brazil

Hardiness Zones USDA 9–10; Sunset 16–17, 21–27

Growing Tips Full sun to partial shade. Moist, fertile soils, but tolerates dry periods. Pinch stems to prevent legginess.

Cultivars and Related Species *Tibouchina grandifolia* generates larger, more rounded, fuzzy leaves, five to nine inches long by three to six inches wide, and has purple-violet flowers.

Companion Plants Mix glory bush with ornamental onions (*Allium*), blue oat grass (*Helictotrichon sempervirens*), the blue-flowered cranesbill *Geranium* Rozanne, *Artemisia* 'Powis Castle', coleus (*Solenostemon scutellarioides*), and shiny, burgundy-leafed *Canna* 'Australia.'

Viburnum | Viburnum

Viburnums contribute good form, clean foliage, often fragrant flowers, and persistent colorful fruit to mixed borders. The lance-shaped to rounded leaves are generally coarse-textured and prominently veined with good fall color, though some species' leaves have beautiful glossy green foliage. Small white to pink-flushed flowers are borne in spherical or domed clusters and are followed by red, black, or blue fruit.

Native Habitat Thickets and woodlands in northern temperate regions

Hardiness Zones USDA 2–9; Sunset 1–11, 14–24, 31–43

Growing Tips Full sun or partial shade. Moist but well-drained soils. Fruiting is often enhanced if several of the same species are planted for cross-pollination.

Cultivars and Related Species American cranberry bush (*Viburnum opulus* var. *americanum*) has showy white flowers and orange to red fruit; deciduous smooth-witherod (*V. nudum* 'Winterthur') is a beauty with very glossy leaves, red to reddish-purple fall color, and white flowers that ripen to a pink and blue fruit combo; in warmer climates, *V. davidii* is an evergreen border shrub three to five feet tall with oval, three-veined leaves and stunning metallic-blue fruit. A selection of the doublefile viburnum, *V. plicatum* f. *tomentosum* 'Summer Snowflake', offers compact habit, continuous flowering, and red autumn fruit. Korean spice viburnum (*V. carlesii*) offers grayish-green foliage and domed pinkish-white flower clusters with exceptional fragrance.

Companion Plants Combine the early-spring bloomers with bulbs, columbines (*Aquilegia*), or spurges (*Euphorbia*). The beautiful fall leaf color and fruits harmonize well with tawny ornamental grasses, hybrid anemones and asters.

Weigela florida | Weigela

This old-fashioned shrub is spreading with arching branches, so give it some space to tumble to the ground. Clusters of rosy-pink, bell- to funnel-shaped flowers (a bit like azaleas) open in great profusion in late spring. Modern cultivars offer better cold hardiness and range of floral (light pink to dark red) and foliage color (burgundy-purple to variegated).

Native Habitat Scrub and woodland margins in northern China, Korea, and Japan

Hardiness Zones USDA 4–8; Sunset 1–11, 14–17, 32–41

Growing Tips Full sun to partial shade. All types of fertile, well-drained soils.

Cultivars and Related Species *Weigela florida* Wine and Roses is a standout

Purple-leafed Wine and Roses is one of the modern selections of weigela that have revived this classic border shrub's popularity.

with dark burgundy-purple foliage and intense rosy-pink flowers. It holds its leaf color best in full sun. For hot color, try red-flowered *W. florida* 'Red Prince' or 'Rumba', which is dark red with a yellow throat; 'Variegata' has pale yellow-green variegated foliage and pink flowers that fade to white. *W. subsessilis* is unique with yellow flowers.

Companion Plants Pinks (*Dianthus*), irises, peonies, and false indigo (*Baptisia australis*) blend well with weigela.

Perennials for Sun

Achillea Hybrids | Hybrid Yarrows

Hybrid yarrows are tough, easy-care perennials that herald summer in the mixed border. Yellow-flowered cultivars are the offspring of fernleaf yarrow (*Achillea filipendulina*). They are vigorous and bear large yellow flowers and handsome gray-green, ferny leaves on two- to three-foot-tall plants. The hybrids derived from common yarrow (*A. millefolium*) guarantee an abundance of flower colors—from rosy hues to deep desert reds—on three-foot stems rising from finely cut green foliage.

Native Habitat Grasslands and garden origin

Hardiness Zones USDA 3–9; Sunset 1–24, 26, 28–45

Growing Tips Full sun. Average, dry to moist, well-drained soil. Deadhead to encourage rebloom. Divide every three years in early spring or fall.

Cultivars and Related Species *Achillea* 'Coronation Gold' is the time-tested grande dame, topping out at three feet, with large heads of bright golden yellow on self-supporting stems; 'Moonshine' has pale yellow flowers that are easier to blend in borders. Anthea is a newcomer sporting a combination of showy, pale yellow to sulfur-yellow flowers on two-foot stems. For earthier tones, try brick-red 'Fireland' or 'Terracotta', which has peachy flowers with a reddish-orange cast.

Companion Plants Yarrows blend nicely with blue-flowered catmints (*Nepeta*), sea hollies (*Eryngium*), and purple- and violet-flowered salvias. They also look at home in meadow plantings with grasses and wildflowers.

Agastache | Giant Hyssop

Giant hyssops are robust nonstop summer bloomers and excellent butterfly feeding stations in the border. They offer a palette of peach, orange, raspberry, amethyst, and blue flower spikes atop two- to four-foot plants. Green to gray-green leaves are toothed and aromatic, often smelling of anise or camphor.

Strong vertical form and long-lasting spikes of flowers in a spectrum of colors make giant hyssops a good choice for hot-hued mixed borders.

Native Habitat Garden origin

Hardiness Zones USDA 5–9; Sunset 4–24

Growing Tips Full sun or light shade. Moist but well-drained, rich soil. Deadhead to prolong flowering.

Cultivars and Related Species *Agastache rupestris* has fragrant fuzzy, narrow leaves and wiry stems topped by whorls of salmon-orange flowers. *A.* 'Blue Fortune' offers long-lasting blue flower spikes; 'Tutti-frutti' sports brilliant rose-pink flowers on three- to four-foot stems; the new selection 'Red Fortune' is a dwarf version of 'Tutti-frutti'.

Companion Plants Giant hyssops blend nicely with other plants in the border. Create painterly combinations with yarrows, fall-blooming asters (*Aster oblongifolius* 'Raydon's Favorite' or *A. novae-angliae* 'Purple Dome'), goldenrod (*Solidago rugosa*), and the dazzling foliage of coleus (*Solenostemon scutellarioides*).

Amsonia hubrichtii
Arkansas Bluestar
Arkansas bluestar is a graceful, fine-textured native perennial for mixed borders. Domed clusters of star-shaped, pale blue flowers lend color in mid- to late spring. This clumping plant grows to three to four feet tall and offers luxuriant narrow, linear summer foliage that turns a stunning yellow to peachy orange in the fall.

Native Habitat Grasslands in central and northeastern U.S.

Hardiness Zones USDA 5–9; Sunset 3–24, 28–33

Growing Tips Full sun or partial shade. Average to rich, moist soil. Tolerates some drought when established.

Cultivars and Related Species Willow bluestar (*Amsonia tabernaemontana*) is another tough U.S. native. It has luxuriant willowlike leaves that turn yellow to fiery orange in autumn and clusters of starry, five-petaled steel- to sky-blue flowers on yard-long stems.

Companion Plants Well suited for meadow borders, Arkansas bluestar blends well with ornamental grasses like switch grass (*Panicum virgatum*), yellow and orange sunflowers (*Helianthus*), meadow rues (*Thalictrum*), Joe-pye weeds (*Eupatorium*), and cutleaf staghorn sumac (*Rhus typhina* 'Laciniata').

Angelica gigas | Korean Angelica
In its first season, this biennial or short-lived perennial forms a basal clump of compound green leaves with contrasting reddish-purple veining. Two-year-old plants produce three- to five-foot

New England asters, such as 'Purple Dome', give a blast of color to the border in early fall, when many other plants are winding down. They intertwine beautifully with black-eyed Susans and goldenrods.

branched flower stems with inflated red-purple leaf sheaths, which open to reveal striking dark purple flowers heads—magnets for bees in late summer and early fall.

Native Habitat Damp woodlands and meadows in northern China, Korea, and Japan

Hardiness Zones USDA 4–9; Sunset 1–10, 14–24, 29–43

Growing Tips Full sun to partial shade. Moist, fertile, loamy soil. Allow to reseed and move about the border on its own, but use a controlling hand.

Cultivars and Related Species Archangel (*Angelica archangelica*) is a roadside weed whose four- to six-foot height, coarse texture, and greenish-yellow flower heads make it a nice focal point in a mixed meadow border; *A. pachycarpa* is a shorter plant with glossy green compound leaves and white flower clusters.

Companion Plants *Angelica gigas* combines nicely with late-season sneeze-weeds (*Helenium*), oxeye (*Heliopsis*), hardy ageratum (*Eupatorium coelestinum*), and asters.

Aster novae-angliae
New England Aster
New England asters explode with billowing clusters of violet-purple daisylike flowers with bright yellow centers from late summer to mid-autumn. The thick stems can rise to six feet and are covered with clasping, lance-shaped leaves. Many selections have been made for larger flower size, color (including pink and rose red), and compact growth.

Native Habitat Moist woodlands from New Mexico to North Dakota east to Alabama and Vermont

Hardiness Zones USDA 3–8; Sunset 1–24, 31–43

Growing Tips Full sun. Average to rich, evenly moist soil with good drainage. Staking is required for taller types. Control height by not fertilizing and shearing plants to half their size in early summer.

Cultivars and Related Species *Aster novae-angliae* 'Purple Dome' is a well-behaved, shorter cultivar to two feet tall with intense purple flowers. Little separates New York asters (*A. novi-belgii*) from their New England relatives; breeding has made the differences even more subtle but expanded the color palette. *A. oblongifolius* 'Raydon's Favorite', my favorite aster, offers lavender-blue flowers when most other plants are finished.

Companion Plants Plant New England asters toward the back of the border with other tall perennials and ornamental grasses. New York ironweed (*Vernonia noveboracensis*), false indigo (*Baptisia australis*), coneflowers (*Echinacea*), and Korean feather reed grass (*Calamagrostis brachytricha*) are great mates.

The native wildflower false indigo is gaining favor as a cultivated border companion to plants like Siberian iris and ornamental grasses.

Baptisia australis | False Indigo

False indigo takes a few years to establish itself in the border, but it is well worth the wait. Vertical smoky-black stems contrast nicely against bluish-green compound (trifoliate) leaves. Mature clumps reach three to four feet tall and wide, with exquisite form and substance. Beautiful purplish-blue (the color of indigo) flowers resembling sweet peas bloom in mid-spring. Blackish-brown, upright inflated seedpods develop after flowering. As they ripen, the loose seeds rattle inside.

Native Habitat Open woods, riverbanks, and sandy floodplains in eastern and southern U.S.

Hardiness Zones USDA 3–8; Sunset 1–24, 28–43

Growing Tips Full sun. Lean to average, well-drained soils. Deadhead to encourage repeat bloom, leaving a few to develop ornamental seedpods.

Cultivars and Related Species New hybrids are propelling false indigos into mainstream gardening. *Baptisia* 'Purple Smoke' offers charcoal-gray stems and blue-purple flowers. *B.* 'Carolina Moonlight' sports beautiful soft yellow flowers. White false indigo (*B. alba*) provides white flowers contrasted against black stems.

Companion Plants False indigos work nicely in the border with other tall, spiky perennials like Siberian iris (*Iris sibirica*) and early cool-season grasses like *Calamagrostis × acutiflora* 'Overdam' or 'Karl Foerster'.

Low masses of airy thread-leafed tickseed are great space fillers among ornamental grasses, ornamental onions, and yarrows.

Coreopsis verticillata
Thread-Leafed Tickseed

Thread-leafed tickseed is stellar in the border, exploding into bloom in early summer with masses of starry one- to two-inch yellow flowers atop well-branched stems covered with finely textured, thread-like foliage. It forms airy clumps that soften the border and contrast nicely with bold, coarse-textured neighbors.

Native Habitat Dry, open woodlands and roadsides from Maryland south to Arkansas and Florida

Hardiness Zones USDA 3–9; Sunset 14–24, 26, 28–45

Growing Tips Full sun to partial shade. Average to rich, moist but well-drained soils. Deadhead to prolong flowering.

Cultivars and Related Species *Coreopsis verticillata* 'Moonbeam' sports soft lemon-yellow flowers and a somewhat lax upright habit; 'Crème Brulee' is a vigorous version of 'Moonbeam' with larger, mustard-yellow flowers that occur all along the stems rather than just above the foliage; 'Limerock Ruby' is a hot new color introduction sporting rosy red, 1½-inch flowers with yellow centers. Its classification as a perennial or annual is still in question. Tall tickseed (*C. tripteris*) is an architectural giant in the border at three to nine feet tall, with big clusters of two-inch starry yellow flowers.

Companion Plants Juxtapose thread-leafed coreopsis with the contrasting blue and purplish-blue flowers of lavenders (*Lavandula angustifolia*), catmints (*Nepeta*), coneflowers (*Echinacea*), or a bluish ornamental switch grass like *Panicum virgatum* 'Heavy Metal'.

Dianthus gratianopolitanus
Cheddar Pink

Their showy floral display and spicy clove scent give cheddar pinks an old-fashioned appeal. They are low growing and form compact mats of spiky gray-green to silvery foliage that often persists through winter. Plant them at border edges where their heady fragrance is most easily enjoyed. Fragrant, deep pink flowers with toothed petals bloom profusely above the foliage. Many choice cultivars have been introduced with various flower forms and shades of color.

Native Habitat Cliffs and rock outcroppings in northwest and central Europe

Hardiness Zones USDA 3–9; Sunset 1–24, 30–45

Growing Tips Full sun. Moist to dry, extremely well-drained alkaline to slightly acidic soils. Divide every two to three years to keep them vigorous. Deadhead to stretch bloom time.

Unlike most other coneflowers, 'Art's Pride', a hot new cross between *Echinacea purpurea* 'Alba' and *E. paradoxa*, has no purple coloring.

Cultivars and Related Species *Dianthus gratianopolitanus* 'Bewitched' has light pink flowers with contrasting magenta eyes and blue-green foliage. *D. amurensis* is mat-forming with deeply toothed, purplish-pink to mauve flowers with dark centers. Carthusian pink (*D. carthusianorum*) is a taller, tufted cluster-headed pink with deep reddish-pink flowers. *D. knappii* is another taller species with solitary sulfur-yellow flowers atop 15-inch stems.

Companion Plants Contrast cheddar pinks with other silvery perennials like *Artemisia* 'Powis Castle' or the large-leafed *Stachys* 'Helene von Stein'. Taller *Dianthus* species blend well with beard tongue (*Penstemon*) and ornamental grasses like purple moor grass (*Molinia caerulea*).

Echinacea purpurea
Purple Coneflower

Purple coneflowers are the native mainstays among summer perennials. Erect,

well-branched flower stems rise two to four feet above coarse, hairy basal foliage. They are topped by dozens of flowers from midsummer to early fall. Stocky, dark cones of fertile disk flowers are surrounded by a showy skirt of drooping red-violet, petallike, sterile ray flowers.

Native Habitat Dry prairies from Michigan and Virginia to Georgia and Louisiana

Hardiness Zones USDA 3–8; Sunset 26–45

Growing Tips Full sun to partial shade. Average to rich loamy soil. Even moisture, but drought-tolerant once established. Cut back flower stems for repeat bloom and to prevent reseeding.

Cultivars and Related Species *Echinacea purpurea* 'White Swan' produces graceful white reflexed flower heads around orange-brown cones. Tennessee coneflower (*E. tennesseensis*) sports upturned dark mauve ray flowers around greenish-pink cones; *E. paradoxa* offers bright yel-

Spiky-leafed, silvery-gray sea hollies provide strong vertical architecture to the mixed border.

low flowers (the paradox!) and rises two to three feet above mostly basal foliage. A new offering, *E.* 'Art's Pride' is a must-have plant with peachy-orange flowers.

Companion Plants Coneflowers are versatile bedfellows in the mixed border but blend particularly well with ornamental grasses like little bluestem (*Schizachyrium scoparium*), perennial phlox, blazing stars (*Liatris*), yarrows (*Achillea*), Russian sage (*Perovskia atriplicifolia*), and salvias.

Eryngium | Sea Holly

Sea hollies add extreme architecture and ghostly presence to the summer mixed border—guaranteed to garner attention! Stout one- to three-foot-tall stems rise above a basal rosette of stiff, spiny leaves generally marked with silvery-white veins. A stiff, spiky collar of silver to sapphire-blue bracts surrounds a thistle-like flower head composed of many tiny white to steel-blue flowers.

Native Habitat Dry, rocky places and coastal areas in Europe, northern Africa, Turkey, China, and Korea

Hardiness Zones USDA 3–8; Sunset 1–24, 29–43

Growing Tips Full sun. Sandy to loamy, well-drained soil; prone to root rot in heavy soils. Some species will thrive in gravel and pure sand. Once established, do not disturb.

Cultivars and Related Species Miss Wilmot's ghost (*Eryngium giganteum*) is a very coarse but dramatic three-foot plant with green flower heads and conspicuous spiny, silvery-gray bracts. Mediterranean sea holly (*E. bourgatii*) grows one to two feet tall with blue-

tinged flower stems and silvery bracts surrounding blue or gray-green cylindrical flower clusters. The hybrid *E.* 'Sapphire Blue' sports large flower heads on sturdy stems of intense steel blue.

Companion Plants Sea hollies make bold statements in the border, so combine them with softer foliage plants like calamints (*Calamintha*), yarrows (*Achillea*), and ornamental oreganos (*Origanum*). See-through perennials like Culver's root (*Veronicastrum virginicum*) make good neighbors.

Erysimum 'Bowles' Mauve' 'Bowles' Mauve' Wallflower

'Bowles' Mauve' wallflower is a time-tested shrubby, evergreen perennial, particularly for West Coast gardens. It makes a mounded, two- to three-foot-tall mass in the border with continuous spikes of mauve to soft purple, four-petaled flowers above beautiful gray-green foliage. It is best grown in regions with cool summers and mild winters.

Joe-pye weed should not be called a weed at all—this hardy native makes a great back-of-the-border foil for other late-summer bloomers like asters, coneflowers, and goldenrods.

Native Habitat garden origin

Hardiness Zones USDA 6–10; Sunset 4–6, 14–17, 22, 23

Growing Tips Full sun. Poor to average, well-drained soils; happy in alkaline soils. Deadhead to encourage continuous bloom.

Cultivars and Related Species *Erysimum linifolium* 'Variegatum' adorns the border with somewhat tufted, yellow and creamy-white variegated leaves and mauve flowers; *E. cheiri* (syn. *Cheiranthus cheiri*) has been long cultivated as a biennial or annual for its sweet-scented yellow, cream, orange, red, brown, or burgundy flowers.

Companion Plants 'Bowles' Mauve' combines very nicely with other gray- and green-foliaged perennials and grasses, including irises, spurges (*Euphorbia*), lamb's ears (*Stachys byzantina*), and blue oat grass (*Helictotrichon sempervirens*).

Eupatorium purpureum subsp. *maculatum* | Spotted Joe-Pye Weed

Native Habitat Wet, swampy areas of northeastern and southeastern U.S.

Hardiness Zones USDA 4–7; Sunset 1–9, 14–17, 28–43

Joe-pye weeds should not be treated as weeds—these hardy natives offer great late-season drama in the back of mixed borders and are guaranteed landing platforms for butterflies, birds, and bees. This species offers sturdy, purple-spotted stems rising to eight feet and supporting large, flat-topped claret-pink flower heads from midsummer to autumn.

Growing Tips Full sun. Moist but well-drained soils. May require staking or other support.

Cultivars and Related Species *Eupatorium purpureum* subsp. *maculatum* 'Gateway' is a shorter, more manageable five- to six-foot-tall plant with huge mauve-pink

The yellow bracts of Mediterannean spurge afford vertical contrast to low-growing bugleweed and barrenwort.

flower clusters atop dark wine-red stems; 'Bartered Bride' grows to eight feet tall and has pure white flowers. *E. rugosum* 'Chocolate' is a three- to four-foot-tall plant with chocolate leaves on deep shiny purple stems and small white flower clusters in early fall; it will tolerate partial shade.

Companion Plants Joe-pye weeds look most natural with other meadow perennials like asters, coneflower (*Rudbeckia nitida*), goldenrods (*Solidago*), and the billowing switch grass *Panicum virgatum* 'Cloud Nine'. They hold their own with other tall natives like New York ironweed (*Vernonia noveboracensis*) and also play nicely with rose mallows (*Hibiscus moscheutos*).

Euphorbia | Spurge

Spurges are structural plants for the mixed border, providing substance and evergreen framework. Many species are succulent, with thick stems and milky

sap, blue-green foliage, and chartreuse-yellow to reddish-orange floral bracts that are quite welcome in early spring. The true flowers are tiny and mostly inconspicuous, but the bracts that surround them literally glow in the border.

Native Habitat Open woods and rocky slopes in temperate regions, the Mediterranean, and tropics

Hardiness Zones USDA 5–9; Sunset 1–10, 14–24, 28–43

Growing Tips Full sun to partial shade. Require little to moderate water, but insist on well-drained soils. Deadhead to control reseeding if needed.

Cultivars and Related Species *Euphorbia characias* subsp. *wulfenii* (Mediterranean spurge) is three to four feet tall, with blue-green foliage and torches of yellow-bracted flowers; *E. myrsinites* (myrtle spurge) has stiff, roundish blue-gray leaves on stems that seem to slither along

The delicate tiny pink blossoms of *Gaura lindheimeri* 'Siskyou Pink' nod gently with the slightest breeze, adding an element of movement to the mixed border along with plumy ornamental grasses.

the ground; *E. polychroma* forms a mound of deep green leaves tipped by bright fluorescent-yellow bracts. A new darling of the spurge scene is *E. dulcis* 'Chameleon', with rich purple foliage contrasting with small yellow-green bracts and flowers. The Caribbean copper plant (*E. cotinifolia* 'Atropurpurea'), with wine-red leaves, thrives in hotter climates (USDA 10–11; Sunset 25, 27) and makes a great container plant elsewhere.

Companion Plants Spurges seem more at home with other Mediterranean-climate companions like rosemarys (*Rosmarinus*), lavenders (*Lavandula*), and red-hot poker (*Kniphofia uvaria*). Spiky plants like yuccas (*Yucca filamentosa*) and rattlesnake master (*Eryngium yuccifolium*) are good bedfellows.

Gaura lindheimeri | White Gaura
You really can't beat this perennial for summer flower power, transparency, and movement in the border. Wiry flower spikes rise above the clumpy foliage, dressed with pink buds that open to one-inch white flowers suffused with pink. The flowers look like swirls of small moths or butterflies as they dance about in the slightest breeze. In fall, the bare flower stems turn reddish brown, easily passing for a brown sedge.

Native Habitat Dry grasslands of Texas and Louisiana

Hardiness Zones USDA 5–8; Sunset 3–39

Growing Tips Full sun. Average, well-drained soils. Deadhead to prevent self-sowing if a problem in your region.

Cultivars and Related Species Several cultivars of white gaura have become popular, with more on the way. Many of the newer selections have been bred for compactness (which I think detracts from the beauty of this stately perennial) and new flower colors. *Gaura lindheimeri* 'Whirling Butterflies' is a free-flowering selection with reddish-pink sepals and heavy swarms of white butterfly blooms atop two-foot stems; 'Siskiyou Pink' offers pink to rosy-red flowers.

Companion Plants Highlight white gaura against a broadleafed evergreen like boxwood (*Buxus*) or holly (*Ilex*). Its wiry, see-through flower stems allow neighborly views of companions like tall meadow rues (*Thalictrum*), Russian sage (*Perovskia atriplicifolia*), ornamental onions (*Allium*), and lamb's ears (*Stachys byzantina*).

Helenium autumnale | Sneezeweed

Sneezeweeds are exceptional "color makers" in late-summer borders. Flowers come in shades of fiery red, burnt orange, copper-brown, and yellow. Upright, three-foot-tall stems are covered with toothed foliage and topped with daisylike flowers reminiscent of small pinwheels. The ray flowers lend color to the brown, pomponlike centers.

Native Habitat Damp meadows and woodland margins in Canada and eastern U.S.

Hardiness Zones USDA 3–8; Sunset all

Growing Tips Full sun. Average, well-drained soils. Deadhead to encourage repeat bloom. May require staking. Foliage prone to powdery mildew and yellows in dry conditions, so you may want to hide the base of the plant with other foliage plants.

Cultivars and Related Species New flower colors keep appearing in the marketplace, each one as tempting as the next. *Helenium* 'Moerheim Beauty' grows to two to three feet and dazzles with dark copper-red ray flowers around a dark

brown disk; *H.* 'Zimbelstern' sports golden-brown-blushed wavy ray flowers around a brown center; *H.* 'Coppelia' is another favorite, with coppery burnt-orange petals.

Companion Plants Sneezeweeds are at home with other late-season flowers like the fall-blooming daylily *Hemerocallis* 'Autumn Minaret', goldenrods (*Solidago*), the tawny-flowered Indian grass *Sorghastrum nutans* 'Sioux Blue', New England asters (*Aster novae-angliae*), and salvias like 'Indigo Spires' or *Salvia guaranitica* 'Black and Blue'.

Helianthus | Sunflower

Hardy, perennial sunflowers easily rival their popular annual relatives. Flowers may be smaller in size, but their numbers are much greater. Sunflowers are tough, tolerant plants that inject color into summer and fall borders just when needed. The flower heads are composed of soft to bright yellow rays surrounding a dark center of many tiny disk flowers. The sturdy, tall stems rarely require staking.

Native Habitat Dry woodlands and prairies in North and Central America

Hardiness Zones USDA 4–9; Sunset 1–24, 28–43

Growing Tips Full sun. Moist, average to rich soil. Once established, quite drought tolerant. Tough and easy to grow, but give them room.

Cultivars and Related Species *Helianthus* 'Lemon Queen' is a stunning hybrid that grows six to eight feet tall and is loaded with cheery lemon-yellow daisylike flowers in late summer; Maximillian sunflower (*H. maximiliani*) tops out at ten feet, with bright yellow three-inch flower heads nestled in axils on the stems in early autumn; willow-leafed sunflower (*H. salicifolius*), is valued for its delicate linear gray-green leaves and slender upright clusters of two-inch flowers in mid-autumn.

Companion Plants Sunflowers combine well with taller perennials at the back of the border, where they help support each other. Perennial phlox, salvias, asters, and ornamental grasses are great mixers. For a more tropical look, combine sunflowers with tall, dark-leafed cannas, such as *Canna* 'Intrigue', castor bean (*Ricinis communis*), and Mexican sunflower (*Tithonia rotundifolia*).

Hemerocallis | Daylily

With more than 30,000 cultivars and counting, there is a flower form—single, double, reblooming, diploid, and tetraploid—and color perfect for lending summer vibrance to your mixed border. These easy-to-grow, dependable perennials sport grassy, strap-shaped leaves and trumpet-shaped flowers—each bloom lasting only a day.

Native Habitat Garden hybrids; species: forest edges, mountains, and meadowlands in China, Japan, and Korea

Hardiness Zones USDA 3–9; Sunset all

Growing Tips Full sun. Average to rich, well-drained soil. Consistent moisture for best foliage, but daylilies grow from thick tuberous roots that make them quite drought tolerant; if foliage yellows, cut to the ground for regrowth. Deadhead regularly and prune out exhausted flower stalks for best appearance. Divide clumps every three years or so.

Cultivars and Related Species *Hemerocallis altissima* (Sunset 3–10, 14–24, 26–34, 39) is one of the tallest and latest bloomers, with fragrant pale yellow flowers on five- to six-foot stems in summer and early fall; *H. citrina* is a three-foot-tall midseason evening bloomer with star-shaped, greenish-yellow flowers that emit a subtle citrus aroma. Rebloomers like *H.* 'Happy

The slender, grasslike stems of Siberian iris remain vertical and green long after the late-spring flowers fade.

Returns' (light yellow) and 'Rosy Returns' (rosy red) are great in the front of the border or in containers; *H.* 'Lady Fingers' has exquisite flower form—spidery blooms in bright greenish yellow.

Companion Plants Daylilies don't come in blue, so companions like Russian sage (*Perovskia atriplicifolia*), catmints (*Nepeta*), and lily-of-the-Nile (*Agapanthus*) are good color blenders. Stunning contrasts in structure are created with sea hollies (*Eryngium*), the brushy spires of *Liatris*, and thread-leafed coreopsis (*Coreopsis verticillata*).

Iris sibirica | Siberian Iris

Among irises, in my opinion, Siberian iris is the best performer in mixed borders in most regions of the country for both flowers and foliage. They produce clumps of narrow, almost grasslike leaves that remain vertical and green through the growing season (most die back in winter). Slender stems up to four feet tall

(depending on the cultivar) each bear two to five blossoms with upright petals (standards) and flaring to drooping, dark-veined petals (falls). The color range spans whites to shades of blue, lavender, purple, wine-red, pink, and light yellow.

Native Habitat Pond and stream margins in central and eastern Europe, Turkey, and Russia

Hardiness Zones USDA 5–8; Sunset 1–10, 14–23, 32–45

Growing Tips Full sun to light, dappled shade. Well-drained, neutral to slightly acidic soil. Divide when clumps show hollow centers.

Cultivars and Related Species *Iris ensata* (Japanese iris) thrives in moist borders, bearing exquisite large, often flattened flowers in solid colors and combinations. Louisiana iris (an iris group of approximately four species with many hybrids) also thrives in damp conditions, particularly in hot-summer regions, with zigzag stems and flowers in most colors. Pacific Coast iris (an iris group of 11 species plus hybrids) suited only for mild regions with winter rain and dry summers, offers evergreen foliage and bloom in early spring in a wide color range, often with attractive veining on the falls.

Companion Plants Combine Siberian iris with shrubs like ninebark (*Physocarpus opulifolius*) or elderberries (*Sambucus*). False indigo (*Baptisia australis*), poppies (*Papaver*), and peonies also bloom concurrently with Siberian iris in the border.

Kniphofia uvaria
Red-Hot Poker, Torch-Lily

Red-hot poker aptly describes the flaming, three- to five-foot-tall torches of drooping tubular flowers that erupt through the mixed border in late spring and early summer—a great perennial for an element of drama. Clumping tufts of long, stiff linear leaves stay closer to the ground and are usually obscured by

neighboring foliage. The flowers vary in color from pure scarlet, orange, yellow, and cream to bicolors and are very attractive to bees.

Native Habitat Moist places in rough grass or along streams in South Africa

Hardiness Zones USDA 5–9; Sunset 1–9, 14–24, 28–34

Growing Tips Full sun. Evenly moist but well-drained soil is a must. In colder climates, mulch plants, but be sure to keep excess mulch and water off the crowns.

Cultivars and Related Species *Kniphofia triangularis* offers linear, grasslike foliage and pokers of reddish orange on wiry stems later in the season. Of the many *Kniphofia* hybrids, 'Little Maid' is a gem at two feet tall, with easy-to-blend, soft yellow flowers. 'Border Ballet' sports cream to pink flowers in late summer; 'Shining Sceptre' tops out at four feet, with large, fat pokers of soft orange to yellow in midsummer.

Companion Plants Red-hot pokers create a dramatic effect among daylilies, globe thistles (*Echinops*), and sea hollies (*Eryngium*), as well as New Zealand flax (*Phormium tenax*), yuccas, and ornamental grasses.

Lavandula × intermedia
Lavender

There is nothing quite like mounds of aromatic lavender in full bloom. Hybrid lavanders (known collectively as lavandins) possess vigor, yielding more robust plants with bolder foliage than parent species. The gray-green, lance- to spoon-shaped leaves have characteristic rolled edges; a very fine silvery

The flaming-torch flower stalks of red-hot poker can contribute unusually vivid color to the late-spring and early-summer mixed border.

covering of gray hair gives the foliage a soft, appealing texture. In summer, long-stalked spikes of perfumed light blue to violet flowers rise well above the foliage.

Native Habitat Garden hybrid

Hardiness Zones USDA 5–9; Sunset 4–24, 30–34, 39

Growing Tips Full sun. Loose, fast-draining soils mandatory. Prune in early spring when new growth is apparent, not before. Deadhead lightly after flowering.

Cultivars and Related Species
Lavandula × *intermedia* 'Grosso' has fat spikes of very deep purple flowers and large leaves; 'Provence' is similar and favored for its fine aromatic quality. *L. angustifolia* 'Hidcote' is a popular compact, two-foot-tall English lavender cultivar with deep purple flowers. *L. stoechas* (Spanish lavender) sports narrow gray-green leaves and fat spikes of pungent, dark purple flowers topped by showy purple bracts.

Companion Plants Combine lavenders with roses, salvias, ornamental oreganos (*Origanum*), and false indigo (*Baptisia australis*).

Leonotis leonurus | Lion's Tail
Lion's tail is a six-foot-tall, back-of-the-border perennial that saves its bloom for autumn to early winter, depending on the climate. For most of the season it is a green plant in the border, quietly gaining size and vigor. The hairy, square stems and lance-shaped leaves with coarsely toothed edges are quite aromatic. Dense whorls of rusty orange, fuzzy, two-inch-long flowers are at their peak in the waning days of autumn

when other border plants are shifting foliage colors to yellows, oranges, reds, and browns.

Native Habitat Upland grasslands and rocky areas in South Africa

Hardiness Zones USDA 8–11; Sunset 8–24

Growing Tips Full sun. Moderately fertile, well-drained soils. Drought tolerant.

Cultivars and Related Species None.

Companion Plants Lion's tail blends beautifully with Indian grass (*Sorghastrum nutans*) and purple moor grass (*Molinia caerulea*). Striking combinations can be had with late-blooming *Salvia* 'Purple Majesty' and the autumn foliage color of bluestars (*Amsonia*).

Monarda didyma | Bee Balm
Bee balms bloom at the height of summer with beautiful spherical flower heads highly attractive to bees and humming-

birds. Flowers appear in terminal whorls on stocky square stems that are sparsely branched. Each bloom has two lips, the upper one hooded and erect, the lower one three-lobed and more spreading. The lance-shaped to oval leaves are mid- to dark green but are often purplish green with conspicuous veins. The foliage is aromatic when crushed.

Native Habitat Moist, open woods, roadsides, and clearings from Maine to Michigan, south to New Jersey and Ohio; mountains to Georgia

Hardiness Zones USDA 3–8; Sunset 2–11, 14–17, 30–41

Growing Tips Full sun or dappled shade. Thrives in wet but well-drained humus-rich soil. Not drought tolerant. Divide clumps every couple of years to control spread and reinvigorate.

Cultivars and Related Species *Monarda* 'Jacob Cline' is highly mildew resistant, with big bright red flowers on stocky two- to three-foot stems; 'Marshall's

Delight' sports true pink flowers on strong stems and also has good mildew resistance; 'Mahogany' grows in three-foot-tall clumps and bears wine-red flowers with brownish-red bracts below the flower head. *M. punctata* (spotted bee balm) is border-worthy for its whorls of purple-spotted, yellow-pink flowers with pink to lavender bracts from midsummer to early autumn.

Companion Plants Bee balms are well suited for wet to moist borders. Combine them with other moisture lovers like Joe-pye weed (*Eupatorium purpureum* subsp. *maculatum*), sneeze-weeds (*Helenium*), and queen-of-the-prairie (*Filipendula rubra*).

Nepeta × *faassenii* | Catmint

Catmint is unbeatable for long summer-time bloom in the mixed border. It is easy-to-grow, low maintenance, and pest resistant. Undulating mounds of soft, gray-green foliage peak at two feet tall. The leaves are aromatic and attractive to cats, which, it must be warned, love to roll in plantings of it. Loose flower spikes cover the plants in a lavender to violet-blue haze for four to six weeks. Shear faded flower spikes in early summer to encourage repeat bloom.

Native Habitat Garden hybrid

Hardiness Zones USDA 4–8; Sunset 1–24, 30, 32–43

Growing Tips Full sun or light shade. Well-drained, sandy to humus-rich soil. Plants can quickly overstep their bounds and engulf neighbors, so deadhead or shear back plants once or twice during season. They will respond with quick regrowth and rebloom.

Catmint is perfect for the front of the border, its blue, butterfly-attracting flower spikes adding height to low mounds of aromatic foliage.

Deceptively delicate looking, penstemons are tough natives adaptable to many growing conditions.

Cultivars and Related Species *Nepeta* 'Walker's Low' is well behaved, forming a dense, wide-spreading 18-inch-tall mound of foliage covered with bluish-purple flowers all season long. *N.* 'Six Hills Giant' is a taller selection with abundant whorled clusters of lavender-blue flowers on three-foot stems. *N. sibirica* 'Souvenir d'André Chaudron' is an upright cultivar of Siberian catmint, with larger leaves than *N.* × *faassenii*, bigger deep blue flowers, and more vertical stems to over three feet tall.

Companion Plants Catmints provide ever-present spots of color in the border. Allow them to spill over border edges onto paths. They are also blenders and color harmonizers. Good companions include roses, spurge (*Euphorbia dulcis*), lady's mantle (*Alchemilla mollis*), and ornamental onions (*Allium*).

Penstemon | Beard Tongue

Penstemons are finally getting more notice. They grow in a wide variety of conditions, and many species are well suited for dry-climate borders, offering persistent, semievergreen basal foliage. The leaf shape of penstemons varies from lance to wiry or needlelike. Tubular, bell-, or funnel-shaped flowers, often reminiscent of foxgloves, appear in a wide range of colors from early summer to fall on branched flower stems.

Native Habitat Open plains to subalpine and alpine areas in North and Central America

Hardiness Zones USDA 2–10; Sunset 1–24, 29–43

Growing Tips Full sun to partial shade. Fertile, but well-drained, gritty soils with

sharp drainage. In cold, moist-winter areas, it benefits from a dry winter mulch.

Cultivars and Related Species *Penstemon digitalis* 'Husker Red' forms maroon-red, semievergreen basal rosettes that shoot up three-foot flower stems with pink-tinted white tubular flowers. *P. barbatus* (beardlip penstemon) sports very narrow, linear leaves on flower stems that can rise to six feet from course basal foliage. Open, airy panicles support pendent tubular red flowers with yellow beards on the lower lip. *P. pinifolius* (pineleaf penstemon) is better suited for the front of the border, where it forms spreading mounds of finely textured, needlelike foliage and bright scarlet or yellow flowers in summer.

Companion Plants Taller penstemons look great with mulleins (*Verbascum*); shorter species combine nicely with low-growing sedums, ornamental oreganos, burgundy-leafed switch grass *Panicum virgatum* 'Shenandoah', and Korean feather reed grass (*Calamagrostis brachytricha*).

Perovskia atriplicifolia
Russian Sage

Russian sage is a striking silver plant excellent for border architecture and accent. It becomes a woody-based perennial or subshrub in Mediterranean climates and is highly useful for its whitish-gray vertical stems covered with gray-green foliage. The leaves are toothed, deeply divided, or delicately cut and very aromatic. In summer, multibranched three- to four-foot-tall spires of two-lipped, tubular flowers form a lavender-blue haze above the foliage.

Native Habitat Rocky sites in Afghanistan and Pakistan

Hardiness Zones USDA 5–9; Sunset 3–24, 28–35, 37, 39

Growing Tips Sun. Well-drained, dry alkaline soils. Performs nicely in coastal areas. Leave dried stems standing for a silvery touch to the winter border. Cut back to six inches in spring.

Cultivars and Related Species There are several cultivars of Russian sage available, but to my mind they all read about the same in the border. *Perovskia atriplicifolia* 'Longin' is upright in habit with sturdy, erect, stems and narrow leaves that are less toothed than other Russian sages; 'Filigran' sports more finely cut foliage.

Companion Plants Russian sage is a nice silvery foil for the dark burgundy-leafed rose mallow *Hibiscus* 'Kopper King' or ninebark *Physocarpus opulifolius* Diabolo. Summer-blooming shrubs like the blue-flowered rose of Sharon *Hibiscus syriacus* 'Bluebird' or pink *Rosa* 'Nearly Wild' show nicely through a lacy thicket of Russian sage stems.

Phlomis | Jerusalem Sage

I love this plant for its sagelike woolly gray-green foliage and vertical stems encircled with whorls of fascinating hooded flowers. Lance-shaped to rounded leaves form basal clumps that hug the ground early in the season and then send up three- to four-foot stems sporting ball-shaped axillary whorls of flowers along the upper half of the stem in summer.

Native Habitat Rocky sites throughout the Mediterranean

Hardiness Zones USDA 4–9; Sunset 3–24, 30–34, 39

Growing Tips Sun. Fertile but well-drained soil. Tolerant of dry conditions in cool-summer regions. Leave dried whorled stems in the winter border for interest.

Cultivars and Related Species *Phlomis fruticosa* (Jerusalem sage) grows to three feet tall with whorls of dark golden-yellow

The tall stems of Russian sage work well toward the back of the border against evergreen shrubs.

flowers; *P. russeliana* (sticky Jerusalem sage) produces basal foliage with rounded to heart-shaped leaves and three-foot flowering stems with whorls of hooded, pale yellow flowers; *P. tuberosa* tops out at four to five feet, with whorls of purple-pink flowers.

Companion Plants Jerusalem sage looks at home with red-hot pokers (*Kniphofia*), New Zealand flax (*Phormium tenax*), and daylilies (*Hemerocallis*). Accent flowering stems against a background of pittosporums, yews (*Taxus*), junipers, or evergreen hollies (*Ilex*).

Phlox paniculata | Perennial Phlox, Summer Phlox

Perennial phlox are mainstays for color, fragrance, and exuberance in the midsummer border. Their flower power is derived from large, dome-shaped clusters (corymbs) of trumpet-shaped flowers in colors ranging from bright white to pink, salmon, and fuchsia to cherry red; blooms of some types have a contrasting eye. Leaves are two to five inches long, narrow and tapering to a slender point. The foliage is subject to powdery mildew, but many proven resistant selections are available.

Native Habitat Moist meadows and riversides in eastern U.S.

Hardiness Zones USDA 4–8; Sunset 1–14, 18–21, 27–43

Growing Tips Sun to partial shade. Well-drained, evenly moist soils—hot, humid weather and poor air circulation in the border can lead to powdery mildew. Deadhead spent flower heads to encourage lateral flowering. Shear plants in half by early to mid-June to control height.

Cultivars and Related Species *Phlox paniculata* 'David' grows vigorously to three to four feet tall with brilliant white flower heads and is highly mildew resistant; 'Bright Eyes' grows only to three feet and has light pink flowers with a red eye zone; 'Robert Poore' has clean foliage all summer and sports medium to deep pink flowers. For more outrageous color, try 'Düsterlohe' ('Nicky'), which has deeply saturated magenta flowers.

Companion Plants Combine perennial phlox with hydrangeas and rose of Sharon (*Hibiscus syriacus*), or contrast them against a backdrop of the purple-leafed ninebark *Physocarpus opulifolius* Diabolo. Mingle them with yarrows (*Achillea*), salvias, and giant hyssops (*Agastache*).

Rudbeckia fulgida | Black-Eyed Susan

The classic black-eyed Susan is a ring of golden-yellow ray flowers around a blackish-brown center composed of many tiny disk florets. *R. fulgida* offers multibranched clusters of these coneflowers from mid- to late summer. This tough-as-nails composite grows up to a yard tall from clumping basal foliage. The five-inch green leaves are slightly hairy and prominently veined.

Native Habitat Moist meadows and open woodlands in eastern U.S.

Hardiness Zones USDA 3–9; Sunset 1–24, 28–43

Growing Tips Full sun. Well-drained, fertile soils. Leave flower heads standing for bird food and winter garden interest.

Cultivars and Related Species Award-winning *Rudbeckia fulgida* var. *sullivantii* 'Goldsturm' grows two to three feet tall with sturdy stems supporting masses of three-inch golden-yellow black-eyed flowers. *R. maxima* (great rudbeckia) offers glaucous gray-green cabbagelike

With over 900 species, there's a salvia suited to virtually any type of gardening condition. *Salvia leucantha* is a beautiful subshrub in dry-climate borders.

basal foliage and beautiful three-inch golden flowers with drooping rays and large blunt cones on six- to seven-foot stems; *R.* 'Herbstsonne' is another giant, rising to six feet with dense flower heads of four- to five-inch bright yellow rays around green to yellowish-brown cones.

Companion Plants Rudbeckias look very natural with shrubs like staghorn sumac (*Rhus typhina*), red-osier dogwood (*Cornus sericea*), and coralbark willow (*Salix alba* var. *vitellina* 'Britzensis'). They are also popular border mates with feather reed grass (*Calamagrostis* × *acutiflora*) and switch grass (*Panicum virgatum*).

Salvia | Sage

With 900-plus species, there is a salvia that meets the height, foliage type, and flower color requirements for any border. In general, salvias have square

stems and aromatic foliage that can be smooth or coarse and sticky. Their colorful summer and fall flowers are characteristically two-lipped, with erect and often hooded upper petals and more spreading lower petals. Flowers appear in branched clusters or whorls in leaf axils, and the colorful calyces persist after petal drop, effectively extending the bloom. Salvias are great hummingbird and butterfly plants.

Native Habitat Sunny sites, dry meadows, rocky slopes, and scrub to moist grasslands in temperate and tropical regions worldwide

Hardiness Zones USDA 5–10; Sunset 2–11, 14–24, 30–41

Growing Tips Full sun; some species tolerate dappled shade. Light to moderately fertile, moist but well-drained soils. Deadhead to prolong flowering.

Cultivars and Related Species *Salvia argentea* (silver sage) forms a spectacular fuzzy mound of silver foliage its first year, followed by spikes of white flowers tinged pink or yellow in its second season. *S. nemorosa* 'Caradonna' is a compact, front-of-the-border sage with 18-inch glowing purple stems covered with deep violet-purple flowers. *S. leucantha* (Mexican sage) is a subshrub in dry-climate borders with arching velvety purple spikes set with small white or purple flowers. *S. uliginosa* (bog sage) is useful in wet borders and sports bright blue flowers.

Companion Plants Fall-blooming salvias are gorgeous companions with fall-fruiting shrubs like beautyberry (*Callicarpa dichotoma*), viburnums, and *Rosa glauca*. For a summer fiesta, combine salvias with riotous bloomers like agastaches, black-eyed Susans (*Rudbeckia*), and perennial phlox.

Sedum | Stonecrop

Sedums lend texture and multiseasonal color to the mixed border. The stems and leaves are fleshy and succulent, usually with a high gloss or blush. Depending on the species, the leaves vary from cylindrical to flattened in shape and may be gray to gray-green, coppery brown to purplish, or yellow. The flowers occur in compound clusters sporting star-shaped, five-petaled flowers in a wide color range.

Native Habitat Mountains of Northern Hemisphere and arid areas of South America

Hardiness Zones USDA 3–10; Sunset 1–24, 28–43

As the summer flowers give way to an autumnal emphasis on structure and textures, 'Autumn Joy' sedum provides a late-season jolt of color.

Growing Tips Full sun. Moderately fertile, well-drained, slightly alkaline soils. Leave the dried flower heads on some of the upright forms for fall and winter interest.

Cultivars and Related Species Ever-popular *Sedum* 'Autumn Joy' has a clumping habit with sturdy, upright unbranched stems and midgreen leaves. Stems are topped with flat heads of deep salmon-pink flowers that shift to russet and coppery red as the season progresses. *S. spectabile* 'Brilliant' sports gray-green leaves and flowers with bright pink petals; 'Neon' is an offspring of 'Brilliant' with deeper rose-pink flowers in thicker clusters. S. 'Purple Emperor' offers dusky purple foliage and mauve-pink flowers; 'Arthur Branch' is my favorite, with reddish stems and coppery-brown foliage. Enthusiasts of variegated varieties will drool over the white-and-green leaves of *S. erythrostictum* 'Frosty Morn'.

Companion Plants Sedums combine with all manner of ornamental grasses, black-eyed Susan (*Rudbeckia fulgida*), lamb's ears (*Stachys byzantina*), and yuccas. Bluebeard (*Caryopteris incana*), ninebark (*Physocarpus opulifolius*), and red-osier dogwoods (*Cornus sericea*) make good shrub backdrops.

Verbascum | Mullein

Mulleins are big, bold perennials that punctuate borders with vertical drama. Most are biennial, producing a rosette of basal foliage in their first season and tall, erect stems bearing dense flower spikes the second year. The leaves are often gray-green to silvery white and softly hairy or woolly. Flowers are saucer-shaped and range in color from white to yellow to pink-violet.

Native Habitat Dry, stony hillsides, wastelands, and open woods in Europe, north Africa, and west and central Asia

Hardiness Zones USDA 4–9; Sunset 3–10, 14–24, 32–34, 39

Growing Tips Full sun. Average to poor but well-drained soil. May require staking. Leave dried brown spires standing for winter interest, but expect reseeding.

Cultivars and Related Species *Verbascum olympicum* grows to seven feet, with densely woolly, gray-white leaves. The six-foot branching flower stems covered in golden-yellow flowers provide a candelabra effect. *V. phoenicium* (purple mullein) sports textured basal foliage that is wrinkled, slightly scalloped on the edges, and wonderfully veined. Slender stems of white, pink, violet, or dark purple flowers can occur. Nettle-leafed mullein (*V. chaixii*) grows to three feet and bears saucer-shaped, pale yellow flowers with purple filaments. Numerous smaller, self-supporting hybrids are being introduced with distinctive flower color, such as four-foot *V.* 'Cotswold Queen', which sports saturated yellow flowers with purple filament hairs; 'Gainsborough' offers a soft yellow in the border.

Companion Plants As they are hybridized for smaller size and expanded color, mulleins are becoming more popular in the mixed border. They complement Jerusalem sages (*Phlomis*), yarrows (*Achillea*), perennial phlox, black-eyed Susans (*Rudbeckia*), salvias, sneezeweed (*Helenium autumnale*), and feather reed grass (*Calamagrostis* × *acutiflora*).

Verbascums like the nettle-leafed mullein have the height, bold flower color, and robust structure to stand as cross-seasonal focal points in the border.

Ornamental grasses, such as the Korean feather reed grass in the background, are valued for the vertical interest and movement they offer as well as for their often colorful, long-lasting plumy inflorescences.

Ornamental Grasses for Sun

Calamagrostis × *acutiflora*
Feather Reed Grass

Feather reed grass is stunning for vertical accent in the border, particularly in mass plantings. It is a cool-season grass that greens up quickly in the spring. The flowering stems rise four to six feet tall and are loosely feathered and subtly purplish when they first appear, but they quickly transform to narrow, vertical, buff-colored plumes. This grass remains upright and attractive through the season even after heavy rains and never requires staking. It rarely produces viable seed and will not compromise adjacent natural areas or properties.

Native Habitat Naturally occurring hybrid

Hardiness Zones USDA 4–9; Sunset 2–24, 29–41

Growing Tips Full sun to partial shade. Well-drained fertile soils with adequate moisture. Tolerates heavy clays. Cut back to about five inches in late winter or early spring.

Cultivars and Related Species *Calamagrostis* × *acutiflora* 'Karl Foerster' has a strict upright habit to six feet; 'Overdam' sports foliage with subtle longitudinal creamy-white stripes and grows only four to five feet tall; 'Avalanche' is a brighter and more vigorous selection than 'Overdam', with broader white striping. *C. brachytricha*, Korean feather reed grass, is a warm-season grass that flowers in early autumn with very beautiful strong reddish-purple-tinted inflorescences that fade to silvery gray.

Companion Plants Feather reed grasses make bold statements when mass planted in large borders. They are attractive with staghorn sumac (*Rhus typhina*), daylilies

Fountainlike *Molinia caerulea* 'Variegata' offers contrast to the heavier foliage of evergreen border shrubs.

(*Hemerocallis*), purple coneflower (*Echinacea purpurea*), perennial phlox, Russian sage (*Perovskia atriplicifolia*) and 'Venusta' queen-of-the-prairie (*Filipendula rubra* 'Venusta').

Molinia caerulea | Purple Moor Grass

This clumping grass produces a green mound for most of the season until wiry, see-through flower stems skyrocket above it in late summer. It has a beautiful arching habit to five feet tall when in flower, lending movement and rhythm in the slightest breeze. It has tiny flower spikelets, purple-tinted when opening, but they are very subtle. Golden-yellow foliage appears in autumn.

Native Habitat Moist heaths, bogs, and mountain grasslands in the British Isles and continental Europe and Asia

Hardiness Zones USDA 4–9; Sunset 2–9, 14–17, 32–41

Growing Tips Full sun to partial shade in regions with hot summers; cool summers produce best growth. Tolerates low soil fertility and both acid and alkaline soils.

Cultivars and Related Species *Molinia caerulea* subsp. *arundinacea* 'Skyracer' is upright to seven feet, with foliage that turns clear gold in autumn; 'Variegata' only grows to two feet, but the leaves are dramatically striped light yellow to creamy white.

Companion Plants Purple moor grass blends well with shrubs like black elderberry (*Sambucus nigra*), rose of Sharon (*Hibiscus syriacus*), and summersweets (*Clethra*). Perennial companions include tall tickseed (*Coreopsis tripteris*), rudbeckias, and red-leafed rose mallow *Hibiscus* 'Kopper King'.

Panicum virgatum | Switch Grass

Germany popularized this native American grass for mixed borders. It is a

Beneath its airy panicles, the graceful blades of 'Shenandoah' switch grass take on a burgundy hue in fall.

long-lived warm-season grass that begins growth in late spring and hits its stride in late summer. Leaf color varies from deep green to powder blue to burgundy-red, depending on the cultivar. The airy flowering panicles are often pink or reddish when first opening. Switch grasses offer a variety of forms, from erect and narrow to lax and billowing. They are very sturdy grasses that should be left standing to enhance the winter border.

Native Habitat Prairies, open woods, and brackish marshes throughout most of the U.S and eastern Canada

Hardiness Zones USDA 4–9; Sunset 1–11, 14–21, 28–43

Growing Tips Full sun. Most soils, from sandy to heavy clay. Withstands soggy conditions. Self-sowing is minimal in border plantings.

Cultivars and Related Species *Panicum virgatum* 'Cloud Nine' is a tall selection that grows to eight feet, with huge billowing inflorescences; 'Heavy Metal' is a beautiful glaucous blue and grows strictly upright to five feet tall and will not take as much space in a mixed border; 'Shenandoah' is unrivaled for its burgundy leaf color, which deepens to dark wine red by autumn.

Companion Plants Switch grasses make excellent backdrops in the mixed border and provide companionship for fall asters (*Aster oblongifolius*), perennial sunflowers (*Helianthus*), bluestars (*Amsonia*), coneflowers (*Echinacea purpurea*), black-eyed Susans (*Rudbeckia*), and salvias.

Phormium tenax | New Zealand Flax

New Zealand flaxes are drama queens in mixed borders, displaying fans of many swordlike, stiff vertical leaves. The reddish-brown flower stalks bear dark red or yellow flower clusters and can grow to nine feet tall by five feet wide in Mediterranean-type climates.

There are many brightly colored leaf forms in a range of sizes. They are also well suited for containers that can be moved about in the border.

Native Habitat Scrub, hillsides, and swamps in New Zealand

Hardiness Zones USDA 9–10; Sunset 7–24

Growing Tips Full sun to partial shade. Likes ample water but tolerates some drought. Can take cool-winter temperatures but not hard frost; overwinter in a frost-free garage or basement—worth the effort, since older plants are more handsome.

Cultivars and Related Species *Phormium* 'Apricot Queen' offers sturdy erect yellow and green leaves. Among the dark-leafed selections are reddish-purple 'Atropurpureum', dark reddish-brown 'Dark Delight', and deep maroon and scarlet 'Dazzler'. Other cultivars have striking stripes and edgings of red, apricot, cream, green, and bronze: 'Flamingo' offers shades of orange, rose, light green, and yellow; 'Pink Stripe' produces bronze-green to gray leaves edged with pink; and 'Maori Sunset' warms the border with apricot to pink tones blending with green.

Companion Plants New Zealand flaxes are at home with red-hot poker (*Kniphofia uvaria*), Jerusalem sage (*Phlomis*), salvias, Russian sage (*Perovskia atriplicifolia*), and any number of colorful cannas.

Yucca filamentosa | Adam's Needle

Yuccas are very architectural and make striking silhouettes in the border. Clusters of tough, lance- to sword-shaped leaves are neatly arranged in rosettes. Nodding, creamy-white bell-shaped flowers appear on big upright compound flower stems. Position yuccas in the border where their sharp, pointed leaves will not do harm to unwary garden strollers.

Native Habitat Dry sandy places from New Jersey to Florida

Hardiness Zones USDA 4–9; Sunset 1–24, 26–43

Growing Tips Full sun. Well-drained soils.

Cultivars and Related Species *Yucca filamentosa* 'Bright Edge' sports spectacular bright golden-edged dark green leaves; 'Color Guard' has leaves with a yellow center stripe edged in green. Dazzling coral color develops along the stripes in colder weather.

Companion Plants Group yuccas with sedums, hens-and-chicks (*Sempervivum*), and low-growing penstemons. They also contrast nicely with bold, tropical foliage

New Zealand flax is a drama queen in the mixed border, offering selections whose swordlike leaves range from dark reds to candy-hued stripes.

California poppies mixed with African daisies add a meadowlike airiness to a mixed border of darker-leafed perennials and shrubs, highlighted with natural and manmade focal points.

plants like cannas, coleus (*Solenostemon scutellarioides*), and taros (*Colocasia*).

Annuals for Sun

Arctotis (syn. *Venidium*) Hybrids
African Daisy

Most of the cultivated South African daisies are perennial hybrids grown as half-hardy annuals in most regions of the country. They have lobed, gray-green leaves that are rough and covered with a soft felt. Cheery, bright three-inch, daisy-like flower heads bloom in white, rose-pink, red, yellow, and tangerine. They bloom most heavily in spring and fall (and into winter where it is warm enough), slowing down in hot summer weather—although newer hybrids have improved heat tolerance.

Native Habitat Garden origin; species: dry, stony places in South Africa

Growing Tips Full sun. Average soils. Water consistently during heavy bloom, then let go drier. The plants survive as perennials in mild climates but tend to bloom more heavily in their first year and are best treated as annuals.

Cultivars and Related Species *Arctotis* 'Wine' offers deep pink flowers; 'Tangerine' sports soft orange flowers; and 'Killerton Red' is aptly named.

Companion Plants Combine African daisies with sedums, red-hot poker (*Kniphofia uvaria*), blue oat grass (*Helictotrichon sempervirens*), or yuccas.

Eschscholzia californica
California Poppy

California poppies are perennials in their native habitat but are cultivated as annuals in most regions. Their foliage is blue-green and finely divided. Single flowers are two inches wide, with satiny orange petals that vary from yellow to deep burnt

Not only do the delicate blooms of flowering tobacco contrast nicely with fuzzy, coarse-leafed silver sage, but the flowers' nighttime fragrance and the sage's shimmering foliage make a great evening-garden duo.

orange. They do not transplant well, so sow seeds where you want plants to grow and then let them reseed and move about your borders. They look great on border edges and along gravel paths and drives.

Native Habitat Coastal areas of California and Oregon

Growing Tips Full sun. Most soil types. Summer water will extend the bloom time. Deadhead flowers if you do not want plants to reseed.

Cultivars and Related Species Garden forms are available in a wide color range—yellow, pink, rose, flaming orange, red, cream, and white. The Silk strain offers bronze-tinted foliage and semidouble flowers in a full color range.

Companion Plants California poppies mix well with smaller clumping ornamental grasses like purple moor grass (*Molinia*

caerulea), blue fescues (*Festuca*), or blue oat grass (*Helictotrichon sempervirens*). Plant them on border edges with sea thrift (*Armeria maritima*) and low-growing sedums.

Nicotiana alata | Flowering Tobacco

Flowering tobacco is grown as an annual or short-lived perennial, depending on your region. It forms a basal rosette of dark green, sticky foliage and tall flower stems to five feet tall with long-tubed greenish-yellow flowers flared at the mouth into five-pointed lobes. Flowers are strongly fragrant in late afternoon and evening during the summer.

Native Habitat Mountain slopes and valley floors in southern Brazil and northern Argentina

Growing Tips Full sun or partial shade. Regular irrigation, particularly during the summer. Deadhead the green cap-

Fragrant banks of trailing, free-flowering *Petunia integrifolia* fill gaps in a sunny border as the plants weave themselves among their neighbors.

sules to encourage side branching and additional bloom.

Cultivars and Related Species *Nicotiana sylvestris* 'Only the Lonely' grows to a statuesque five-foot-tall plant with dense clusters of nodding, intensely fragrant white flowers; *N. langsdorffii* is a graceful plant with nodding tubular lime-green bells. *N. mutabilis* offers enchanting nodding flowers that begin white, age to pale pink, and fade to deep rose pink. Hummingbirds find it fascinating.

Companion Plants Contrast flowering tobacco against an evergreen hedge or shrub grouping. They look splendid interspersed with perennial phlox, daylilies (*Hemerocallis*), dahlias, and switch grass (*Panicum virgatum*).

Petunia | Petunia

Hybrid multiflora petunias are riding a new wave of popularity. They have been bred for neat, compact growth, better heat and rain tolerance, and smaller (two-inch) and more numerous flowers. They are ideal for filling gaps at the front of mixed borders when companion bulbs and perennials have faded or gone dormant. Petunias offer a spectrum of color, including white, pink, red, pale yellow, and violet-blue, and they frequently have an intoxicating fragrance.

Native Habitat Garden hybrid; species: stony slopes and disturbed ground in South America

Growing Tips Full sun. Average soil. In midsummer, cut back rangy plants by about half for new growth and flowering.

Cultivars and Related Species In addition to the hybrid multifloras, try some of the old-fashioned species petunias. *Petunia integrifolia* is a miniature with one-inch, bright pink flowers with deep lavender throats. It is a trailing petunia and will weave through neighboring plants without strangling them. *P.* 'Rainmaster' sounds modern but dates back to the early 1800s. The white two-inch blooms are heavenly scented, and the plant is more upright than trailing, growing to two feet tall.

Companion Plants Plant petunias alongside lady's mantle (*Alchemilla mollis*), lamb's ears (*Stachys byzantina*), or *Artemisia* 'Powis Castle' at the front of the border.

Tagetes patula | French Marigold

Small-flowered, trouble-free French marigolds continue to have a place in mixed borders. They are generally robust and dependable, and the handsome and long-lasting flowers come in a color parade of pale yellow through gold to orange and maroon. Flowers may be sin-

'Torch' is a robust, bushy cultivar of Mexican sunflower that requires less staking than the species and holds its own with other hot-colored plants toward the back of the border.

gle or fully double; many are distinctly bicolored. They are strongly scented, as is the divided ferny foliage.

Native Habitat Hot, dry slopes and valley bottoms from New Mexico to Argentina

Growing Tips Full sun. Tolerates drought conditions.

Cultivars and Related Species *Tagetes patula* 'Striped Marvel' grows to two feet tall with mahogany stripes on bright yellow petals; *T. lemmonii* (USDA 8–9; Sunset 8–10, 12–24, 27–29) is a three- to four-foot shrubby perennial marigold that hails from southeastern Arizona, Mexico, and Central America and has fernlike, four-inch leaves that are a fragrant blend of marigold, mint, and lemon, with flowers of golden orange; *T. tenuifolia* (signet marigold) has a finer filigree foliage and smaller one-inch carnation-like flower heads but is incredibly prolific and good for border edges.

Companion Plants Combine marigolds with ornamental grasses, spurges (*Euphorbia*), and artemisias, as well as dark-leafed cannas, castor bean (*Ricinus communis*), and coleus (*Solenostemon scutellarioides*).

Tithonia rotundifolia
Mexican Sunflower

Mexican sunflower is robust, quick growing, and great for vertical effect and hot color. Punctuate the middle and back zones of a border with this husky six-foot-tall, velvety-leafed giant, which flowers with spectacular three- to four-inch flower heads of glowing orange-scarlet ray flowers surrounding yellow centers.

Native Habitat Thickets and scrub from Mexico to Central America

Growing Tips Full sun. Average to poor soils. Tolerates heat and can withstand some drought. Stems are inflated and hollow and will sometimes break or bend in heavy rains and wind—so stake plants or support them in the company of sturdy neighbor perennials and shrubs.

Cultivars and Related Species *Tithonia rotundifolia* 'Torch' is a dense, lower-growing, bushier selection to four feet that may be easier to support.

Companion Plants Combine Mexican sunflower with other true perennial or annual sunflowers (*Helianthus*), burgundy and red-leafed cannas or castor bean (*Ricinus communis* 'Carmencita'), or the hot magenta *Phlox paniculata* 'Düsterlohe' ('Nicky').

Zinnia angustifolia | **Mexican Zinnia**
Mexican zinnias love hot weather and provide peak color in July and August. They can be grown as perennials in areas with mild climates. The bright orange flowers vary from 1 to 1½ inches in size on erect, bushy plants to two feet tall. The two- to three-inch linear to lance-shaped leaves are covered in bristly hairs.

Native Habitat Scrub and desert grassland in southeast U.S. and Mexico

Growing Tips Full sun. Good garden soil. Fertilize generously during growth. Subject to powdery mildew in foggy or very humid places and with overhead irrigation. Use drip irrigation if possible. Provide good air circulation.

Cultivars and Related Species Another small-flowered gem is *Zinnia tenuifolia* 'Red Spider', which grows to two feet carrying masses of rich scarlet flowers with scalloped petals. Other hybrid zinnias are making it to the gardening marketplace: the Profusion series offers 12- to 15-inch-tall bedding zinnias in a nice color assortment.

The heirloom *Allium schubertii* is but one of dozens of colors, sizes, and shapes of ornamental onions.

Companion Plants Zinnias complement ornamental grasses like feather reed grass (*Calamagrostis* × *acutiflora*), lavenders, coleus (*Solenostemon scutellarioides*), and silvery mugworts (*Artemisia*).

Bulbs for Sun
Allium | **Ornamental Onion**
The variety of height, bloom size, and color makes ornamental alliums perfect for the mixed border. Most are planted in fall and begin growth in early spring. Foliage is generally compact and low to the ground, and leafless stems from six inches to five feet tall or more support usually spherical flower clusters. Alliums bloom from late spring through summer in white and shades of pink, rose, violet, red, blue, and yellow. Many look like Christmas ornaments perched on sticks, and some are delightfully fragrant.

Native Habitat Dry, mountainous areas in Northern Hemisphere

Both bulbines (left) and cannas, such as the stripe-leafed, orange-flowered 'Pretoria' (right), are summer bloomers and combine well with other "hot-color" flowers and foliage plants, both annuals and perennials.

Hardiness Zones USDA 4–9; Sunset 1–24, 28–43

Growing Tips Full sun or partial shade, in deep, rich sandy loam. Plant bulbs in fall. Lift and divide after they become crowded; control unwanted seedlings.

Cultivars and Related Species *Allium karataviense* (Turkestan allium), sits low to the ground with five-inch dense round spheres of ivory-white florets with purple-pink highlights in early spring. Broad, flat, bent or backward-curved leaves are edged in red. *A. hollandicum* 'Purple Sensation' features four-inch globes of vivid reddish-purple, star-shaped florets. An heirloom, *A. schubertii,* produces a 12-inch, rose-purple flower cluster resembling a Fourth of July sparkler—guaranteed to grab attention. Drumstick allium (*A. sphaerocephalon*) has dense, dark crimson-purple, egg-shaped flowers and is a great naturalizer in the border.

Companion Plants Ornamental onions look great waltzing with white gaura (*Gaura lindheimeri*), lavenders, and spurges (*Euphorbia*), or accented against smoke bush *Cotinus coggygria* 'Royal Purple'.

Bulbine frutescens | Bulbine
This member of the lily family offers succulent lance-shaped, nine-inch-long blue-green basal leaves. The star-shaped yellow-orange flowers are borne throughout the summer on stems 6 to 12 inches long. It is treated as an annual in most regions, but in warmer zones it will develop a persistent woody-stemmed base.

Native Habitat Desert grasslands of South Africa

Hardiness Zones USDA 9–10; Sunset 14–24

Growing Tips Sun to partial shade in hot-summer regions. Consistent moisture during active growth; keep on dry side in winter. Tolerant of poor, dry soils but will perform best in well-drained, sandy loam.

Cultivars and Related Species *Bulbinella* species are valuable for winter color in warm Mediterranean climate regions, where they are perennial. They are clump forming with narrow, floppy leaves topped in mid- to late winter with four-inch-long spikes of clear-yellow flowers.

Companion Plants Combine these gems with New Zealand flax (*Phormium tenax*), yuccas, giant dracaena (*Cordyline australis*), and spurges (*Euphorbia*).

Canna | Canna

Cannas have big, bodacious foliage and generally hot-colored flowers. The one- to two-foot paddle- to sword-shaped leaves are rich green to bronzy red with selections that have rich veining and variegation. The flowers bloom above foliage on three- to six-foot stalks, in colors varying from white to ivory, pink, yellow, orange, coral, and red. Bicolor and spotted flowers are also available.

Native Habitat Forest margins and moist, open areas in tropical North and South America

Hardiness Zones USDA 7–10; Sunset 6–9, 12–32

Growing Tips Full sun to partial shade. Rich, loose, well-drained soil. Likes hot, humid summers. Water heavily during bloom. Where not hardy, treat as an annual or dig the tuberous clumps in the fall and store in a cool, dark basement.

Cultivars and Related Species *Canna* 'Intrigue' has exquisite deep purple-red leaves with dark veining and small

orange orchid-type flowers; 'Striata' (syn. 'Pretoria') offers bright green and heavily gold-striped foliage with glowing orange flowers; Tropicana sports vividly variegated leaves of bright yellow, glowing orange, and red on a dark purple background with bright orange flowers. 'Stuttgart' produces salmon flowers against stunning variegated leaves of white with patterns of gray, green, and silver—it must be grown in the shade.

Companion Plants Cannas look at home with many perennials and annuals. Their quick growth and bold foliage can create seasonal backdrops for daylilies (*Hemerocallis*), yarrows (*Achillea*), perennial phlox, salvias, coleus (*Solenostemon scutellarioides*), giant hyssops (*Agastache*), and flowering tobacco (*Nicotiana*).

Crocosmia Hybrids
Hybrid Crocosmias

For bursts of torrid summer color, you can't beat *Crocosmia*. Iris-like, pleated leaves grow from small underground corms and develop wiry spikes of brightly

Group tropical-looking crocosmias for a spicy accent, or contrast them with cool-colored plants.

colored, funnel-shaped flowers in hot colors—red, orange, and yellow. They make excellent cut flowers and are favorites with hummingbirds.

Native Habitat Grasslands in South Africa

Hardiness Zones USDA 5–10; Sunset 5–24, 28–39

Growing Tips Full sun to partial shade. Well-drained soils. Require little water once established. In cooler regions where hardiness is questionable, cover with a generous layer of mulch over winter, dig corms for winter storage, or treat as an annual.

Cultivars and Related Species *Crocosmia* 'Lucifer' flowers are upward-facing and bright devilish red. It grows to four feet tall and is one of the hardiest crocosmias (USDA 5). *C. × crocosmiiflora* 'Solfatare' grows to two feet and has bronzy green foliage and rich apricot flowers; 'Emily McKenzie' has bright orange flowers with a red halo surrounding the yellow throat.

Companion Plants Plant crocosmias in clumps and let them punctuate groupings of summer perennials like catmints (*Nepeta*), prairie coneflower (*Ratibida pinnata*), and sneezeweeds (*Helenium*). Accent them against dark-leafed plants like rose mallow *Hibiscus* 'Kopper King' or ninebark *Physocarpus opulifolius* Diabolo.

Dahlia Hybrids | Hybrid Dahlias
It's hard to imagine a late-summer or fall border without dahlias. There is a tremendous diversity of flower types— singles, pompons, cactus, anemones, orchids—and sizes, which range from two inches to over ten inches. The "dinner plate" dahlias are certainly impressive, but I think miniatures and small sizes are most appropriate for borders. Colors span the spectrum except for true blue. The height of dahlias ranges from foot-high bedding types to six-foot-tall plants. Modern dahlias have strong stems, long-lasting blooms that face outward, and attractive green to reddish-black foliage.

Native Habitat Garden hybrids; species: Mexico and Guatamala

Hardiness Zones USDA 8–10; Sunset 6–9, 12–32

Growing Tips Full sun, with light afternoon shade in hot regions. Regular watering. In cold-winter regions, treat as annuals or dig tubers after tops turn yellow or are frosted. Cut tops to four inches, dig clumps, shake off loose soil, and store indoors where it is dry and cool.

Cultivars and Related Species *Dahlia* 'Bishop of Llandaff' has almost black,

Famous for the immense variety of flower types and sizes, hybrid dahlias also offer selections with outstanding foliage, such as 'Bishop of Llandaff'.

Abyssinian sword lily is a late-blooming gladiolus species with up to ten fragrant flowers on each stem.

fernlike foliage and fiery red, single blooms; 'Arabian Night' offers dark maroon-black flowers to three inches in diameter; 'Forncett Furnace' offers sizzling-hot orange-red flowers with a golden eye; 'Kingston Queen' sports deep burgundy foliage and nice apricot flowers centered with deep orange and a yellow eye on four- to five-foot stems.

Companion Plants Dahlias shine when many of the ornamental grasses are in fall bloom. Combine them with switch grass (*Panicum virgatum*) or Korean feather reed grass (*Calamagrostis brachytricha*), or partner them with other tender plants like cannas, coleus (*Solenostemon scutellarioides*), and giant hyssops (*Agastache*) to achieve great color play.

Gladiolus | Gladiolus

Gladiolus adds an element of surprise to border designs. Plant the corms between perennial clumps—they don't take up a lot of horizontal space and will probably surprise you when they thrust through

the border. All glads have sword-shaped leaves and tubular, flared, or ruffled flowers on one-sided flower spikes. They come in almost all colors but blue. Newer selections have sturdy stems that stand upright without staking; individual flowers can approach eight inches across on stems four to five feet tall. But for mixed border designs, I recommend the miniature to small-size glads that grow to three feet tall with spikes of 15 to 20 flowers so they don't overwhelm.

Native Habitat Garden hybrid

Hardiness Zones USDA 8–10; Sunset 4–9, 12–24, 29–33

Growing Tips Full sun. Rich sandy soils, but will grow in any good garden soil. Regular water. In cold-winter regions, treat glads as annuals or dig corms in fall and store in a cool, frost-free, dry place.

Cultivars and Related Species *Gladiolus callianthus* (Abyssinian sword lily) is an excellent border bulb that blooms in late summer and autumn. It grows two to three feet tall and produces two to ten fragrant, creamy-white flowers marked with chocolate-brown blotches at the base of petals. *G. tristis* is dainty and suited for border edges. It has wiry stems to 18 inches topped with creamy-white to pale yellow funnel-shaped flowers veined purple. Its early-spring blooms have an intoxicating nighttime fragrance.

Companion Plants Combine glads with summer bloomers like perennial phlox, yarrows (*Achillea*), and catmints (*Nepeta*). Plant them in front of dark foliage to make their colors zing.

Narcissus | Daffodil

What would a spring border be without daffodils for that early dose of yellow, white, orange, and pink? These bulbous plants bloom in early and mid-spring, and then the foliage slowly yellows and goes dormant until the cycle is repeated the following year. Daffodil foliage is strap-shaped and bright green to glaucous; the flowers are composed of petals that surround a trumpet or cup in the center.

There are three things to note when planning their placement in the border: Many daffodils are fragrant and invite close encounters; the opening blooms usually face the sun; the foliage slowly dies back after blooming and hence needs the camouflage of emerging perennials.

Native Habitat Garden hybrids

Hardiness Zones USDA 2–9; Sunset 1–24, 28–45

Growing Tips Sun to partial shade. Average, well-drained soils. Let foliage die back naturally; if you are extremely fastidious, bundle the leaves in a loose knot close to the ground.

Cultivars and Related Species There are 12 horticultural classes of *Narcissus*. Among my favorites for mixed borders are Cyclamineus types that are very early to bloom, like *N.* 'February Gold' (golden yellow), 'Tête-à-Tête' (golden yellow), and 'Jenny' (white with lemon-yellow trumpet). The Triandrus hybrids bloom later with clusters of medium-size, slender, cupped flowers. 'Thalia' is stellar, with up to three white, beautifully proportioned orchidlike flowers per stem. 'Hawera' is exceptional for mixed borders because of its multiflowering, long-lasting, lightly scented pale canary-yellow flowers with slender foliage that is not a nuisance after flowering.

Companion Plants Daffodils bloom along with a few other bulbs like Siberian squill (*Scilla siberica*) and blend with the emerging foliage of spurges like *Euphorbia polychroma*. Accent them against the colored stems of red-osier dogwood (*Cornus sericea*) or coral bark willow (*Salix alba* var. *vitellina* 'Britzensis').

The overlapping bloom times of blue squills, *Narcissus* 'Tête-à-Tête,' and the large-cupped *N.* 'Ice Follies' ensure weeks of early-spring cheer.

Shrubs for Shade

Aralia elata | Japanese Angelica Tree

This is no doubt one of the most exquisite spreading shrubs for elegant foliage texture. It is very slow growing but well worth the time and patience (and cost for the variegated forms!). The gigantic, tropical-looking compound leaves range from 3 to 5½ feet in length, with individual green leaflets that may turn yellow to orange or reddish purple in the fall. White compound flowers 12 to 18 inches in diameter appear in August, followed by purplish fruit.

Native Habitat Mountain woodlands in eastern Asia

Hardiness Zones USDA 4–8; Sunset 2–24, 28–41

Growing Tips Partial shade. Not particular about soils. Variegated cultivars are usually grafted on rootstock of *Aralia elata* or *A. spinosa,* so remove undesirable suckers that sprout from the base.

Cultivars and Related Species *Aralia elata* 'Variegata' has leaflets strikingly bordered with creamy white; 'Aureovariegata' bears leaflets that are broadly and irregularly edged in yellow.

Companion Plants Japanese angelica tree likes center stage in the border. Underplant with low-growing perennials or groundcovers like pigsqueak (*Bergenia cordifolia*), hostas, or dark-leafed bugleweeds like *Ajuga reptans* 'Chocolate Chip'.

Camellia sasanqua | Autumn Camellia

Autumn camellia in bloom is a plant of great beauty, and its smaller size and finer texture make it more adaptable for mixed borders than its Japanese relative, *Camellia japonica*. Its lustrous dark green leaves set off fall flowers that range in color from white to pink, rose, red, and

With its huge compound leaves, elegant Japanese angelica tree gives the border a tropical touch.

almost every combination in between, and come in single, double, and peony forms.

Native Habitat Woodland areas in China and Japan

Hardiness Zones USDA 7–9; Sunset 4–9, 12, 14–24, 26–32

Growing Tips Partial shade. Moist, acid, well-drained soils rich in organic matter. Prune after flowering.

Cultivars and Related Species *Camellia sasanqua* 'Yuletide' has an upright habit and lustrous dark green foliage with single red flowers around yellow stamens; 'Jean May' offers large, shell-pink semi-double to double flowers; 'Setsugekka' sports white semidouble blooms with large ruffled petals.

Companion Plants Use camellias as accents or focal points or espalier them

The evergreen autumn camellia 'Yuletide' grows into a compact pyramid that reaches up to ten feet in height and blooms from fall into winter.

Hardiness Zones USDA 4–8; Sunset 2–10, 14–17, 28–41

Growing Tips Partial shade for best leaf variegation, but grows in full sun. Tolerates many soil types; moist soils. Adapts well to urban conditions, particularly air pollution.

Cultivars and Related Species None

Companion Plants *Eleutherococcus sieboldianus* 'Variegatus' mixes nicely with lady fern (*Athyrium filix-femina*) and Christmas fern (*Polystichum acrostichoides*), Allegheny spurge (*Pachysandra procumbens*), and dark-leafed coral bells like *Heuchera* 'Amethyst Myst' and 'Plum Pudding'.

against a wall or fence at the back of the border. They combine well with the silver-leafed coral bells *Heuchera* 'Silver Scrolls' or Japanese painted fern (*Athyrium niponicum* var. *pictum*), as well as yellow-leafed Hakone grass (*Hakonechloa macra* 'Aureola'), and lungworts (*Pulmonaria*).

Eleutherococcus (syn. *Acanthopanax*) *sieboldianus* 'Variegatus' Variegated Five-Leaf Aralia

Shimmering variegated foliage characterizes this fast-growing deciduous shrub, perfect for lightening up a shady border with a tropical appearance. This plant's habit is upright, with arching stems four to six feet high with an equal spread. The palmate compound leaves of five to seven green leaflets are edged with creamy white. The light brown stems have slender prickly spines underneath leaf nodes, so beware!

Native Habitat Scrub and woodlands in eastern China

Itea virginica | Virginia Sweetspire

Virginia sweetspire is a valuable shrub in the mixed border for its showy upright to drooping flower spikes and subtle fragrance in May and June, after many other shrubs have had their spring fling. This suckering, deciduous shrub has dark green summer foliage that shifts to spectacular reddish purple with hints of orange and yellow in autumn, offering an excellent fall-color alternative to the popular but invasive burning bush (*Euonymus alatus*).

Native Habitat Wet, swampy areas of eastern U.S. from Missouri and Louisiana to New Jersey and Florida

Hardiness Zones USDA 5–9; Sunset 3–6, 26, 28, 31–39

Growing Tips Partial or dappled shade to full sun—very adaptable. Moist but well-drained, fertile soils. Easy to grow.

Cultivars and Related Species *Itea virginica* 'Henry's Garnet' is a three- to five-foot

North American native Virginia sweetspire will spread freely across the border. Give it plenty of room or carefully monitor its growth.

selection with showy six-inch-long chains of white flowers in early summer. The foliage turns wine-red in fall; Little Henry is a low-mounded, compact sweetspire to 30 inches with great fall color.

Companion Plants Combine Virginia sweetspire with other plants that thrive in moist conditions, such as *Ligularia dentata,* Japanese iris (*Iris ensata*), and sedges like *Carex glauca* or *C. siderosticha* 'Variegata'.

Hydrangea macrophylla
Bigleaf Hydrangea

Bigleaf hydrangea is a time-honored deciduous shrub four to six feet tall, with bold foliage and brightly colored mophead flower clusters. It commands love and attention in summer borders. The waxy dark green leaves are coarsely toothed and up to eight inches long.

Snowball, or hortensia, types have mostly sterile flowers with large, colored sepals. Lacecaps sport flattened flower clusters with small fertile central flowers surrounded by showy sterile flowers. The blossoms last up to four weeks and go through color shifts as they age.

Native Habitat Woodlands in Japan

Hardiness Zones USDA 5–9; Sunset 3–9, 14–24, 26, 28–33, 34

Growing Tips Partial shade or morning sun with plenty of moisture. Deep, moist, organic, well-drained soils. Flower buds are overwintered on previous year's growth, so be careful not to prune them off. Some selections are blue flowered in acid soils, pink in high pH (alkaline) soils.

Cultivars and Related Species *Hydrangea macrophylla* 'Mariesii Perfecta' (syn. 'Blue

Wave') and 'Nikko Blue' are prolific bloomers with large blue to deep lavender mopheads; 'Forever Pink' offers big pink mopheads. For leaf variegation, try 'Maculata' (syn. 'Variegata'), with cream-and-green-patterned leaves and mauve flowers, or 'Lemon Wave', for its variable blend of yellow, cream, and white leaves and mauve lacecaps. A close relative, *Hydrangea serrata,* is smaller, more refined, and has better cold tolerance; 'Blue Billow' will dazzle with its great quantities of intense violet-blue lacecaps. Be on the lookout for a whole range of new hydrangeas with great foliage and new flower forms from Japan, including *H. involucrata*, sporting velvety leaves, compact habit, and lilac-blue lacecaps.

Companion Plants Bigleaf hydrangeas harmonize nicely with the foliage and tall flower spires of black snakeroot (*Actaea racemosa*) and groundcover plantings of coral bells (*Heuchera*), foamflowers (*Tiarella*), hostas, and ferns.

Kerria japonica | Japanese Kerria

Japanese kerria is an underused free-flowering shrub whose open, airy frame-work and texture makes it easy to com-bine with perennials, grasses, and bulbs in mixed borders. It offers multiseason interest—bright golden-yellow, five-petaled flowers in early spring with some repeat in summer, bright green leaves, and yellowish-green stems for winter color. It has an arching habit and grows three to six feet tall and wide.

Native Habitat Thickets and woodlands in China and Japan

Hardiness Zones USDA 4–9; Sunset 2–21, 30–41

Growing Tips Partial or dappled shade on border edges; also grows in full sun. Moist, fertile soils; tolerates periodic flooding but also adaptable to dry soils. Prune out older stems to maintain vigor and encourage green stem color.

Cultivars and Related Species Though it's hard to resist the voluptuous, ball-shaped, double-flowered selections like 'Pleniflora', to my mind, the single-flowered form of *Kerria japonica* is most natural in appearance and easiest to blend in border designs: 'Honshu' is a gem, with large, rich yellow single blooms that overlap on the stems; 'Kin Kan' offers yellow- and green-striped stems with single yellow flowers.

Companion Plants Japanese kerria looks stunning with underplantings of Siberian bugloss (*Brunnera macrophylla*), eastern bleeding heart (*Dicentra eximia*), Lenten rose (*Helleborus orientalis*), or giant wood fern (*Dryopteris goldieana*).

Early-spring flowers grace Japanese kerria, whose airy shape is accented by bright foliage all through summer and greenish-yellow stems in winter.

Changing with age and the seasons, the evergreen leaves of Oregon grape-holly give the spreading or upright plant a new look every few months.

Mahonia aquifolium
Oregon Grape-Holly, Oregon Grape

Oregon grape-holly is a very useful broad-leafed evergreen for border compositions. The coarse, glossy green compound leaves are divided into five to nine leaflets with spiny, hollylike edges. In spring, new growth is an attractive ruddy bronze that sets off the gleaming, sulfur-yellow flowers, which are followed by blue-black, grapelike fruit clusters. Oregon grape-holly grows from three to six feet or more, with a coarse, erect, layered habit and spreads slowly by underground stems.

Native Habitat Woodlands from British Columbia south to northern California

Hardiness Zones USDA 6–9; Sunset 2–12, 14–21, 31–41

Growing Tips Partial shade. Moist, acid, well-drained soils. Shelter from winter sun and drying winds.

Cultivars and Related Species *Mahonia bealei* (leatherleaf mahonia) is a taller shrub, to 12 feet, with strong vertical architecture and compound leaves to more than a foot long divided into 7 to 15 thick, leathery leaflets, fragrant yellow flowers, and powdery-blue berries in erect terminal clusters. *M. repens* (creeping mahonia) grows to three feet tall and has a low spreading habit, spiny bluish-green leaves, yellow flowers, and blue fruits.

Companion Plants Use Oregon grape-holly as a dark foil for early-flowering daffodils (*Narcissus*), hellebores, and anemones. Later in the season, the fruits are spectacular accented with underplantings of variegated sedges like *Carex siderosticha*

'Variegata', or *C.* 'Silver Sceptre'. Large, blue-leafed hostas like *Hosta sieboldiana* var. *elegans* are also stunning.

Pieris japonica | Japanese Pieris

Japanese pieris is a broad-leafed evergreen shrub that deserves consideration in any shady border with moist soil. It slowly develops a dense, tiered shape, 9 to 12 feet tall, which is softened when the shrub blooms. The late-winter flower buds appear like strings of tiny greenish to pinkish-white beads. In spring, they open to pendulous clusters of white, urn-shaped, lily-of-the-valley-like flowers with a light fragrance. New leaf growth can be bright red to bronzy pink, depending on the cultivar.

Native Habitat Forested hillsides in Japan, Taiwan, and eastern China

Hardiness Zones USDA 5–8; Sunset 3–9, 14–17, 31–35, 37

Growing Tips Partial shade. Moist, acid, well-drained soil high in organic con-

Spring-blooming Japanese pieris is a lovely compact evergreen shrub for a moist woodland border.

tent. Shelter from drying winter winds. Remove spent flowers.

Cultivars and Related Species *Pieris japonica* 'Dorothy Wyckoff' is a compact form four to six feet tall, with dark red flower buds that open to white; 'Mountain Fire' produces excellent fire-engine-red color on new growth in spring. *P. floribunda* (mountain pieris) is a much smaller shrub, two to six feet tall, with a broad mounded shape and flowers in upright panicles.

Companion Plants Japanese pieris is at home with early-spring bloomers like bloodroot (*Sanguinaria canadensis*), foamflowers (*Tiarella*), wood anemone (*Anemone sylvestris*), and Lenten rose (*Helleborus orientalis*).

Rhododendron
Rhododendron and Azalea
Of this huge genus of evergreen and deciduous shrubs, many rhododendrons (and azaleas) have a place in mixed borders, but they are fussy about having well-drained organic soil. Most rhododendrons sport spectacular, sometimes strongly scented, rounded clusters (trusses) of stunning white, pink to red, or lavender to purple flowers. But there is a host of species and hybrids in exciting shades of yellow, gold, orange, vermilion, and salmon. For cultivated gardens, rhododendrons are divided into five groups: large-leafed evergreens, small-leafed evergreens, tropical *Vireya* rhododendrons, deciduous azaleas, and evergreen azaleas. Choose your plants based on plant size and hardiness for your region.

Native Habitat Forest to alpine tundra worldwide, particularly North America, China, Tibet, Myanmar, Korea, and Japan.

Hardiness Zones USDA 4–9; Sunset 4–6, 15–17 34, 37, 39

Growing Tips Partial to dappled shade. Acid, organically rich, moist soils with excellent, fast drainage.

Cultivars and Related Species Deciduous azaleas and rhododendrons are color makers in spring borders. *Rhododendron mucronulatum* (Korean rhododendron) grows four to eight feet tall and blooms on naked stems with pinkish-purple flowers in early spring. *R. schlippenbachii* (royal azalea) is six to eight feet tall and very handsome, with soft pink, fragrant flowers arriving before the foliage; the leaves may turn vibrant yellow, orange, and red in autumn. Native *R. vaseyi* (pinkshell azalea) blooms with trusses of funnel-shaped, rose-pink to white flowers before the foliage. For summer bloom, a group of deciduous, hardy azaleas are now available, including *R.* 'Pink and Sweet', a four-foot shrub with loose clusters of strongly scented pink flowers. For evergreen foliage, *R. yakushimanum* (Yakushima rhododendron) grows slowly into a dense mound three feet tall and wide and will not overstep its bounds in the border.

Companion Plants Rhododendrons and azaleas are lovely with small bulbs like grape-hyacinths (*Muscari*) and squills (*Scilla siberica*) at their feet. Partner them with lungworts (*Pulmonaria*), coral bells (*Heuchera*), or large-leafed hostas like *Hosta sieboldiana* var. *elegans* or *H.* 'Sum and Substance'.

Perennials for Shade

Actaea (syn. *Cimicifuga*)
Bugbane, Snakeroot
Bugbanes are summer- to fall-blooming perennials with tall, slender arching wands of bottlebrush-like flowers. The clump-forming basal foliage is ferny and finely textured. White or cream flowers,

occasionally pink tinged, each with two to five small petals and prominent tufts of stamens, cover the flower spikes. Flowers on some species are sweetly fragrant; others are unpleasant. They are followed by greenish-white fruits that fade to a persistent brown for winter interest.

Native Habitat Moist, shady grassland, woodlands, and scrub in northern temperate regions of eastern North America, Russia, China, Mongolia, Korea, and Japan

Hardiness Zones USDA 3–9; Sunset 1–7, 17, 32–45

Growing Tips Partial shade. Moist, fertile, humus-rich soils.

Cultivars and Related Species *Actaea racemosa* (black snakeroot), the earliest to bloom, is a clump-forming native plant with dark green basal leaves and two-foot stems of unpleasantly scented white flowers in midsummer; *A. japonica* var. *acerina* (maple-leaf bugbane) forms dark green basal leaves with 15-inch upright stems of pinkish-white flowers; *A. simplex* 'Brunette' is a fall bloomer with very dark, brownish-purple foliage and stems and compact spikes of purple-tinted, off-white flowers. *A. racemosa* 'Hillside Black Beauty' sports the darkest purplish-black foliage of all.

Companion Plants Mix bugbanes with yellow-leafed Hakone grass (*Hakonechloa macra* 'Aureola'), hostas, coral bells (*Heuchera*), toad lilies (*Tricyrtis*), and evergreen shrubs.

Anemone × *hybrida*
Hybrid Japanese Anemone
This crowning jewel of the autumn border can have single, double, or semidouble flowers on two- to four-foot stems

above three- to five-lobed leaves covered with soft hairs. The branched flower stems bear white to pale pink to rose-burgundy flowers for three to four weeks from late summer to mid-autumn. Japanese anemone hybrids are well adapted to gardens in northern and western regions.

Native Habitat Garden hybrid; species: Afghanistan, Myanmar, China, Japan

Hardiness Zones USDA 4–7; Sunset 3–24, 30–39, 41

Growing Tips Partial shade or sun. Moist, fertile, humus-rich soils.

Cultivars and Related Species *Anemone* × *hybrida* 'Honorine Jobert' is an old-fashioned flower with single white petals and golden-yellow stamens that blooms from late summer to mid-autumn; 'September Charm' has nice, uniform pale pink flowers from midsummer to fall. The grapeleaf anemone *A. tomentosa* 'Robustissima' is a vigorous grower with

mauve-pink flowers and blooms earlier than other Japanese anemones—good for colder regions with early frost dates.

Companion Plants Anemones mix well in the border with hostas, hydrangeas, and autumn snakeroot (*Actaea simplex*).

Aquilegia | Columbine

Columbines welcome spring with 65 different species and a multitude of named varieties that flower for up to a month, particularly in cool weather. They have distinctive rolled petals, sometimes with long spurs. Flower color and form vary tremendously, especially with the hybrids, and some can be quite ostentatious; I prefer the simplicity of North American native species. Columbines are promiscuous and will hybridize naturally in your borders—let them.

Native Habitat Meadows, open woodlands, and mountains throughout the Northern Hemisphere

Hardiness Zones USDA 3–8; Sunset 1–10, 14–24, 32–45

Growing Tips Bright shade produces best flowering but will grow in full sun. Reasonably rich, well-drained soil.

Cultivars and Related Species *Aquilegia canadensis* (wild columbine) is a native beauty bearing simple red and yellow flowers with hooked spurs; *A. chrysantha* (golden columbine) has yellow flowers with long, distinctive spurs; *A. vulgaris* (European columbine) provides a huge range of colors, flower shapes, and sizes. This species includes the doubles and triples of the Barlow series.

Companion Plants Columbines mingle well with other early bloomers like bar-

Flowering in late summer to early fall, hybrid Japanese anemone really shines in a border of soft pastel tones.

Plant wild columbine where you can admire its intricate early-spring flowers up close. It will seed itself politely around the border and is easily transplanted.

renworts (*Epimedium*) and bleeding hearts (*Dicentra*). They also work well with foliage plants like coral bells (*Heuchera*) and spotted dead nettle (*Lamium maculatum*) cultivars.

Aralia racemosa | Spikenard

This big, bold-leafed perennial lends an exotic, tropical air to mixed borders, particularly moist, wet ones. It spreads by underground rhizomes, which produce five-foot-tall stems with long, two- to three-foot leaves divided into many coarse leaflets. Large open umbels of small greenish-white flowers appear in summer, followed by spherical, dark purple fruits that are eagerly eaten by birds.

Native Habitat Mountain woodlands of southwestern, central, and eastern North America

Hardiness Zones USDA 5–9; Sunset 2–24, 28–41

Growing Tips Partial shade. Moist, fertile, humus-rich soils. Shelter from wind.

Cultivars and Related Species *Aralia cachemirica* is a suckering, shrublike perennial with two-foot-long compound leaves and panicles of creamy-white flowers in many small umbels that become fleshy black fruits.

Companion Plants Spikenard mixes well with other shade lovers like ferns, lungworts (*Pulmonaria*), coral bells (*Heuchera*), and toad lilies (*Tricyrtis*).

Astilbe × arendsii
Hybrid Astilbe, False Spiraea

These long-blooming, durable perennials with ferny foliage are very useful in the summer border. Hybrid astilbes can grow up to four feet tall and offer striking, plumed flowers in a wide range of colors ranging from red, pink, and violet-purple to white. The flower heads dry to decorative shades of brown and are attractive throughout the fall and winter.

Native Habitat garden hybrids; species: moist sites in mountain ravines, woodlands, and along streambanks in North America and Southeast Asia

Hardiness Zones USDA 4–8; Sunset 1–7, 14–17, 32–45

Growing Tips Partial shade. Rich, consistently moist, acid soils. Divide and replant every three to four years to maintain vigor and flower quality.

Cultivars and Related Species *Astilbe × arendsii* 'Cattleya' is three feet tall with pink-rose flowers and an open, graceful habit; 'Bridal Veil' is a beautiful white. *A. thunbergii* 'Morheim's Glory' is an impressive four-foot-tall cultivar with glorious light pink blooms. A favorite of mine is *A. chinensis* var. *taquetti*

'Superba.' This hairy plant rises to five feet tall with in-your-face conical plumes of magenta to reddish-purple flowers. Alternatively, *A. chinensis* var. *pumila* makes a good groundcover, growing to 15 inches and producing deep purple compact flowers.

Companion Plants The feathery flowers and ferny foliage of astilbes are beautifully accented by large-leafed pigsqueak (*Bergenia*), Siberian bugloss (*Brunnera macrophylla*), hostas, umbrella leaf (*Darmera peltata*), and rodgersias.

Astilboides tabularis | Astilboides
This big, bold perennial has large, elegant lobed leaves that can reach a whopping three feet across. The foliage rises on long petioles to about five feet tall and looks like green parasols in a shady border or near water's edge. In early to midsummer, the plant bears plumelike panicles of numerous tiny, creamy-white flowers, very reminiscent of astilbes.

Native Habitat Moist woodlands on banks of lakes and streams in eastern Asia

Hardiness Zones USDA 5–7; Sunset 2–9, 14–17, 32–41

Growing Tips Partial shade. Cool, moist, humus-rich soils; will not tolerate submersion or waterlogged conditions.

Cultivars and Related Species There are no cultivars, but it is closely related to *Rodgersia* and in fact was once classified as *R. tabularis.*

Companion Plants The giant leaves of *Astilboides tabularis* contrast well with the finer foliage of bleeding hearts (*Dicentra*) and ferns, as well as the arching stems of Japanese kerria (*Kerria*

Hot-hued astilbes, such as *A. chinensis* 'Purple Lance', are perfect for a splash of bright summer color in a shady corner.

Looking lovely in the company of grasses and ferns, masterwort lightens up the border in early to midsummer with an impressive display of colorful bracts—rather unusual among shade plants.

japonica) and the burgundy flower heads of Korean angelica (*Angelica gigas*).

Astrantia major | Masterwort

It's not so much the flowers of masterwort that are significant but the papery collars of bracts that surround them. Appearing in early to midsummer, the bracts may be green-veined white or occasionally tinted pink or red and surrounding small green, pink, or deep red, five-petaled flowers that resemble pincushions. Masterwort grows one to three feet tall above three- to seven-lobed basal leaves.

Native Habitat Subalpine woods and meadows in central and eastern Europe

Hardiness Zones USDA 4–7; Sunset 3–9, 14–24, 31–41

Growing Tips Partial shade to morning sun if given ample moisture; variegated leaf forms require more light. Moist, fertile, humus-rich soils. Likes cool summers and dislikes hot, humid weather.

Cultivars and Related Species *Astrantia* 'Hadspen Blood' is aptly named for its dark red papery bracts and flowers; 'Shaggy' (syn. 'Margery Fish') sports elongated bracts of creamy white with green tips and deeply cut leaves; 'Sunningdale Variegated' has leaves edged in creamy yellow and pale pink bracts—best in cool-summer regions.

Companion Plants *Astrantia major* is at home with ferns, hostas, and cranesbills such as *Geranium* Rozanne or 'Dilys'.

Athyrium | Athyrium

This versatile fern genus adds style, class, and refinement to the mixed shade border. Handsome crowns of feathery foliage are vigorous and dependable, with fronds of light green to silvery

Rather than form clumps, the painted fern *A.* 'Branford Rambler' is a frisky traveler in the border.

Companion Plants *Athyrium* mixes with everything and anything in the shady mixed border. Some classic combinations include hostas, coral bells (*Heuchera*), foamflowers (*Tiarella*), yellow wax-bells (*Kirengeshoma palmata*), Siberian bugloss (*Brunnera*), and bugbanes (*Actaea*).

Brunnera macrophylla
Siberian Bugloss, Heartleaf Brunnera

This rhizomatous perennial is valued for its bright blue, forget-me-not-like spring flowers followed by two- to eight-inch wide, softly hairy, heart-shaped foliage. It makes a beautiful mounded ground-cover, especially the white and creamy-yellow variegated forms, which help lighten up a green shade border.

Native Habitat Woodlands in the Caucasus region of eastern Europe and northwestern Asia

Hardiness Zones USDA 3–7; Sunset 1–24, 31–45

Growing Tips Partial shade. Moderately fertile, humus-rich, moist but well-drained soils. Consistent moisture is key, otherwise leaf margins discolor.

Cultivars and Related Species *Brunnera macrophylla* 'Hadspen Cream' has irregular creamy-white leaf margins that are most vibrant on new spring growth; 'Langtrees' is grown for its pattern of silver-white spots. A stunning newer cultivar, 'Jack Frost', sports a pattern of silver veins with a dusting of silver over the whole leaf.

gray-green, often with reddish midribs and petioles. There are many species and cultivars displaying a wide variety of foliage colors, patterns, and sizes (some fronds can reach four feet if given the right conditions).

Native Habitat Moist woods and forests in temperate and tropical regions worldwide

Hardiness Zones USDA 3–8; Sunset 1–9, 14–24, 31–43

Growing Tips Partial to heavy shade; likes early-morning sun. Moist, fertile, neutral to acid soil enriched with leaf mold or compost.

Cultivars and Related Species *Athyrium filix-femina* (lady fern) forms bright green leaves throughout the season for a continuously fresh look. *A. niponicum* var. *pictum* (Japanese painted fern) has technicolor fronds that are often gray suffused with reddish, blue, and pink hues; 'Lady in Red' has bright red petioles and midribs. Hybrid *Athyrium* 'Ghost' sports silvery-white fronds.

With leaves that are up to two feet in diameter, umbrella leaf is a showstopper, especially when paired with plants with strap-shaped foliage.

Companion Plants The ephemeral white flowers of bloodroot (*Sanguinaria canadensis*) and snowdrop anemone (*Anemone sylvestris*) play off emerging foliage of the variegated selections. Siberian bugloss also works well as a groundcover under Japanese kerria (*Kerria japonica*) or in a simple interplay with a dark-leafed bugleweed like *Ajuga reptans* 'Chocolate Chip'.

Darmera peltata (syn. *Peltiphyllum peltatum*) | Umbrella Leaf

The curious flowers of umbrella leaf appear before the foliage, in mid- to late spring, as spheres of numerous five-petaled, white to bright pink flowers on naked stems, looking much like an ornamental onion. The leaves that follow are the real show, however—rounded, deeply lobed, and dark green to two feet in diameter, particularly if given lots of moisture. They may turn red in autumn.

Native Habitat Mountain woodlands and moist streamsides from southwest Oregon to northwest California

Hardiness Zones USDA 5–9; Sunset 1–7, 14–20, 32, 34, 36–37

Growing Tips Partial shade; full sun if given ample moisture. Prefers moist, boggy soils; will grow in much drier conditions but not to same dimension.

Cultivars and Related Species None.

Companion Plants The big round leaves of umbrella leaf play off the strappy or grasslike foliage of other moisture lovers like Japanese iris (*Iris ensata*), a yellow-leafed sweet flag such as *Acorus gramineus* 'Oborozuki', sedges (*Carex*), and rushes (*Juncus*).

Dryopteris | Wood Fern, Male Fern

These tough, adaptable ferns are distinctive and eye-catching. The emerging shuttlecock-like foliage opens to beautiful compound fronds and helps to blend and knit companion perennials, annuals, bulbs, and shrubs in shady mixed border designs.

Native Habitat Rocky woodlands and by streams and lakes in temperate regions of the Northern Hemisphere

Hardiness Zones USDA 3–9; Sunset 4–9, 14–28, 31–45

Growing Tips Partial to full shade; moist but well-drained acidic, humus-rich soils.

Cultivars and Related Species *Dryopteris erythrosora* (autumn fern) is a slow-creeping rhizomatous fern of copper-bronze to pinkish-red young fronds that turn shiny, dark green in summer and reach to two feet. *D. goldieana* (giant wood fern) is a robust grower with arching pale green fronds to four feet tall;

Barrenworts are delicate, airy groundcovers perfect for difficult spots like dry shade areas under trees. The foliage of red barrenwort, pictured here, is bronzy red around the leaf margins when it emerges.

the outstanding *D. pseudofilix-mas* (Mexican male fern) has erect fronds to four feet tall; it tolerates higher altitudes under moist conditions.

Companion Plants Wood ferns make striking accent plants in shady borders, and they also mix well with hostas, Solomon's seal (*Polygonatum biflorum*), fairy bells (*Disporum flavum*), and wood anemone (*Anemone nemorosa*).

Epimedium | Barrenwort

Barrenworts are tough, reliable perennials for mixed borders. They make choice groundcovers in difficult areas, such as dry shade under trees. Their small saucer- to cup-shaped flowers in yellow, beige, white, pink, red, or purple often have spurs. They appear in early spring before and as the new heart-shaped compound foliage emerges. Some barrenworts are deciduous; others retain their leathery leaves through the winter.

Native Habitat Woodlands, scrub, and shady, rocky places from Mediterranean to temperate eastern Asia

Hardiness Zones USDA 5–8; Sunset 1–9, 14–17, 31–43

Growing Tips Best in morning sun with afternoon shade. Tolerates dry conditions after establishment. Fertile, humus-rich, moist but well-drained soils. Needs deep winter mulch in cold-winter regions.

Cultivars and Related Species *Epimedium grandiflorum* (longspur barrenwort) has pale pink flowers with long spurs; 'Lilafee' offers beautiful lilac flowers. *E.* × *rubrum* (red barrenwort) has red flowers and new foliage suffused with bronzy red around the leaf margins. *E.* × *versicolor* 'Sulphureum' sports butter-yellow blooms and is among the earliest barrenworts to bloom.

Companion Plants Barrenworts mingle nicely with early-blooming bulbs like squills (*Scilla siberica*) and winter aconite (*Eranthis hyemalis*). Pair them with ferns, bleeding hearts (*Dicentra*), lungworts (*Pulmonaria*), and dwarf goatsbeard (*Aruncus aethusifolius*).

Geranium | Cranesbill

Long-lived, undemanding, and versatile, cranesbills can be trailing, spreading, or mat-forming. There are also taller, clump-forming species that are great mixed border plants. Herbaceous, semi-evergreen, or evergreen, the rounded to palmately lobed leaves can be beautifully marked, textured, or colored. *Geranium* flowers are white, pink, purple, or blue. The saucer- or star-shaped blooms often have contrasting veins and are borne in loose clusters over the foliage.

Native Habitat Varied habitat, except wet areas, throughout temperate regions worldwide

Hardiness Zones USDA 3–8; Sunset 2–9, 14–24, 30–41

Growing Tips Partial shade. Moderately fertile, well-drained soils. Shear in early summer to encourage new growth and flowers.

Cultivars and Related Species *Geranium* 'Ann Folkard' has chartreuse leaves with rose-red to magenta flowers and is a true scrambler, growing through and over small shrubs and neighboring perennials; Rozanne forms a mound of foliage topped by a nonstop display of blue flowers. *G. phaeum* 'Samobor' has leaves splotched in red-purple, accompanied by deep purple flowers; *G. sanguineum* var. *striatum* (bloody cranesbill) is tough as nails, grows to a foot tall, and is covered with veined pink flowers for six to eight

weeks in the spring. *G. maderense* is a robust, evergreen geranium for warmer regions (USDA 8–9, Sunset 14–24). It is a biennial with rosettes of deeply lobed leaves and a profusion of flat, pinkish-magenta flowers in big, imposing clusters.

Companion Plants Coral bells (*Heuchera*), bleeding hearts (*Dicentra*), and sedges (*Carex*) are just a few of the plants that can be combined with cranesbills.

Heuchera | Coral Bells

The perennial plant industry has gone crazy for coral bells—and for good reason! Coral bells are fantastic shady border plants that form clumps and mounds of rounded to heart-shaped, lobed and often toothed leaves in a multitude of variegation and shades. Their charm is their foliage, but they also form loose racemes of small white to pink flowers that rise on stalks as high as two feet above the leaves. The majority of new introductions are hybrids.

Low-mounding with delicate flower stalks, coral bells are famous for foliage as variable as coppery yellow, bronze, and purple with silver veining.

Native Habitat Woodland and rocky areas in North America and Mexico

Hardiness Zones USDA 4–8; Sunset 1–11, 14–24, 31–45

Growing Tips Partial shade to full sun, depending on region; leaves most vibrant with two to three hours of morning sun. Fertile, moist but well-drained soils. Lift and reset crowns if plants begin to push above soil surface, particularly after winter heaving.

Cultivars and Related Species *Heuchera micrantha* 'Palace Purple' is a bronze-leafed standard, but now it has competition. *H. americana* 'Dale's Strain' has silver- or red-mottled leaves with greenish-white flowers. *H.* 'Silver Scrolls' is deep purple overlaid with silver veining. *H.* 'Amber Waves', a new variety, is coppery yellow with red, orange, and peach highlights. *H. villosa* (hairy alumroot) blooms in fall; its cultivar 'Autumn Bride' is particularly striking, forming a mound of lime-green leaves.

Companion Plants Coral bells are very versatile. They mix with hostas, sedges (*Carex*), Siberian bugloss (*Brunnera macrophylla*), toad lilies (*Tricyrtis*), and lady ferns (*Athyrium filix-femina*).

Hosta | Hosta, Plantain Lily

Hostas are queens of the shade! These bold-leafed accent or groundcover plants brighten up dark, shady borders. The leaves may be rounded, heart- or lance-shaped, and their colors, patterns, textures, and sheens are almost infinite—green, blue-green, yellow-chartreuse; solid, variegated; pleated, puckered, cupped; glossy, glaucous. The flower stems are one-sided and will face the brightest light. Blooms appear in summer and range from white to pale lilac to deeper lavender.

Native Habitat Sunny cliffs, rocky stream-sides, woodlands, and alpine meadows in eastern Russia, China, Korea, and Japan

Hardiness Zones USDA 3–8; Sunset 1–10, 12–21, 28, 31–45

Growing Tips Partial shade, but tolerates more sun in northern regions. Fertile, consistently moist but well-drained soils. Tolerates drought, but mulch in summer to retain moisture. Control slugs and snails and protect from deer browse.

Cultivars and Related Species *Hosta plantaginea* is an all-time favorite, with light green leaves and trumpet-shaped, long-tubed white, fragrant flowers. *H. sieboldiana* var. *elegans* is an imposing specimen hosta with rounded, heart-shaped leaves that are puckered and glaucous gray-blue. Award-winning *H.* 'Sum and Substance' is a background hosta that can grow 30 inches tall and 60

For a festival of varied textures, shapes, and foliage colors, combine a variety of the seemingly infinite number of hosta species and cultivars.

Its striking maplelike foliage makes kirengeshoma a fabulous accent plant. The waxy flowers emerge in late summer and early fall.

inches wide, with big, glossy yellow-green leaves and pale lilac flowers; 'Patriot' has round to heart-shaped, slightly cupped leaves that are olive green with irregular white margins and flowers of lavender blue. For the space conscious, *H.* 'Ginko Craig' is a ten-inch-tall hosta with narrow, lance-shaped dark green leaves with clear white edges.

Companion Plants Hostas go with just about everything in the shady mixed border. A few possibilities include cranesbills (*Geranium sanguineum* and *G. maculatum*), Lenten roses (*Helleborus*), bleeding hearts (*Dicentra*), astilbes, and bugbanes (*Actaea*).

Kirengeshoma palmata
Kirengeshoma, Yellow Wax-Bells

Kirengeshoma is a beautiful colony-forming woodland perennial to four feet tall with light green, maplelike leaves and loose clusters of yellow, nodding tubular bells. The flowers are thick and waxy and appear in late summer and early autumn on arching, reddish-purple stems. When not in bloom, kirengeshoma is an unbeatable foliage perennial for shady mixed borders.

Native Habitat Woodlands in Japan

Hardiness Zones USDA 5–8; Sunset 3–9, 14–24, 31–35, 37, 39

Growing Tips Partial shade. Acid soils enriched with leaf mold or other organic matter. Protect from hot afternoon sun and shelter from wind.

Cultivars and Related Species
Kirengeshoma koreana (Korean wax-bells) is nearly indistinguishable to my eye and serves the same function in the border.

Companion Plants Hostas, foamflowers (*Tiarella*), Christmas fern (*Polystichum acrostichoides*), and lady fern (*Athyrium filix-femina*) are all good company for kirengeshoma.

Ligularia | Ligularia, Leopard Plant

Ligularias have large attractive, kidney-shaped to rounded, often toothed leaves on long petioles. The flowers are daisy-like and bloom in orange or yellow clusters on tall, narrow spires. This moisture-loving perennial needs a wet, shady spot in the border or beside a stream or pond where it has room to grow to its potential—it can reach three to five feet tall with a three-foot spread.

Native Habitat Moist grasslands, wet scrub, and mountainous woodland streambanks in central and eastern Asia

Hardiness Zones USDA 4–8; Sunset 3–9, 15–17, 32, 34, 35–41

Growing Tips Partial shade; avoid hot afternoon sun. Moderately fertile, reli-

The delicate foliage and flowers of catmint set off statuesque *Ligularia* 'The Rocket', whose flowers are echoed by the pink spikes of an astilbe.

aged. As the stem elongates and the foliage unfurls, flower buds open to reveal creamy-white to purple tubular to bell-shaped flowers dangling from each leaf node. The arching, angular stems grow three to five feet tall, depending on species, and lend a wonderful rhythm to borders. The fall foliage is bronzy to amber and the berrylike fruits are red or blue-black.

Native Habitat Woodlands in temperate regions of North America and Eurasia

Hardiness Zones USDA 3–8; Sunset 1–7, 14–17, 28–43

Growing Tips Full or partial shade, preferably with two to three hours of bright light in the morning. Well-drained, humus-rich soils.

Cultivars and Related Species Native *Polygonatum biflorum* (small Solomon's seal) is upright and grows two to five feet tall and bears lovely dangling white flowers in pairs or threes at the leaf nodes. *P. odoratum* 'Variegatum' (variegated fragrant Solomon's seal) is a European version with white variegated leaves that complement the aromatic white flowers. It is not as vigorous and grows to a less imposing two to three feet in the border.

Companion Plants Mix Solomon's seal with Allegheny spurge (*Pachysandra procumbens*), Christmas fern (*Polystichum acrostichoides*), hostas, and barrenworts (*Epimedium*).

ably moist soil—wilts quickly if deprived of water. Shelter from strong winds.

Cultivars and Related Species *Ligularia dentata* 'Desdemona' or 'Othello' (golden groundsel) both have leaves that are heart-shaped at the base, with dark purple leaf stalks, veins, and undersides. The flat flower heads are orange-yellow with brown centers. *L.* 'The Rocket' sports triangular to heart-shaped, deeply serrated leaves and lemon-yellow flowers on long four- to six-foot spires.

Companion Plants Ligularias mix well with other moisture lovers like marsh marigolds (*Caltha palustris*), primroses (*Primula*), sedges (*Carex*), Japanese iris (*Iris ensata*), and cardinal flower (*Lobelia cardinalis*).

Polygonatum | Solomon's Seal
Solomon's seal bursts from the ground in spring like a fat asparagus spear with stem and leaves neatly tucked and pack-

Polygonum (syn. *Persicaria*) Fleeceflower, Knotweed
There are several species of *Polygonum* that make good mat-forming, wander-

ing, or weaving border plants and don't share the aggressive, invasive behavior of Japanese knotweed (*Polygonum cuspidatum*). All have white, pink, or red flowers on thin spikes or panicles. Individual flowers are funnel-, bell-, or cup-shaped, followed by distinctive brownish-red, roughly triangular fruits.

Native Habitat Variety of habitats worldwide

Hardiness Zones USDA 4–9; Sunset 2–9, 14–17, 31–43

Growing Tips Partial shade (afternoon best), but tolerates full sun with consistent moisture. A few species tolerate dry soils.

Cultivars and Related Species *Polygonum bistorta* (bistort) is the most widely planted species. It is a vigorous clump-forming species to two feet tall with rounded, wavy, boldly veined green leaves and bottlebrush spikes of pink flowers above them. *P.* 'Red Dragon' has vibrant burgundy, mint-green, and silver leaves. It is a weaver in the border but noninvasive. *P. polymorphum* is four to five feet tall with amazing white plumes of long-lasting flowers—a superb accent plant.

Companion Plants Plant smaller species of *Polygonum* under hydrangeas and box-woods (*Buxus*). The larger knotweeds mix with hostas, coral bells (*Heuchera*), and larger-leafed cranesbills such as *Geranium psilostemon* and *G.* 'Ann Folkard'.

Pulmonaria | Lungwort
Valued for their early flowers and striking foliage, lungworts have rounded to strap-shaped leaves that are often attractively spotted, splashed, or streaked with white or silver. The tiny funnel-shaped flowers bloom in shades of pink, red, violet, purple, blue, or white. After lungworts finish flowering, the summer leaves develop to reveal their dazzling markings and colors for the remainder of the season.

Native Habitat Mountains, moist sub-alpine woodlands and streamsides in Europe and Asia.

Hardiness Zones USDA 4–8; Sunset 1–9, 14–17, 32–43

Growing Tips Full or partial shade. Humus-rich, fertile, moist but well-drained soils. Prune out yellowing flower stems as summer foliage develops.

Cultivars and Related Species *Pulmonaria longifolia* subsp. *cevennensis* (longleaf lungwort) has very silvery strap-shaped leaves to two feet long; *P. rubra* 'Bowles' Red' (red lungwort) offers plain green, almost diamond-shaped leaves and brick-red to salmon-red flowers; *P. saccharata*

The gracefully arching stems of Solomon's seal are a wonderful structural element for the border.

In this springtime border, *Rodgersia aesculifolia* offers superb foliage contrast with ferns and grasses, and pink and white tulips presage the cream to pink palette of its summer-blooming flower clusters.

(Bethlehem sage) sports elliptic, white-spotted midgreen leaves that are short and wide, with funnel-shaped flowers of red-violet, violet, or white with dark green calyces; 'Mrs. Moon' offers beautiful white-spotted foliage after flowering. *P.* 'Majesté' sports leaves that are nearly solid silvery white.

Companion Plants Lungworts grow well with a number of other shade plants; they are lovely nestled near fothergillas, hydrangeas, or rhododendrons. Mix and contrast them with a variegated broad-leafed sedge like *Carex siderosticha* 'Variegata', the Siberian bugloss (*Brunnera macrophylla*) cultivar 'Jack Frost', or burgundy-leafed bugbanes such as *Actaea simplex* 'Brunette'.

Rodgersia | Rodgersia

This big, bold, beautiful plant has unparalleled foliar character. The coarse green leaves, which often assume a bronzy sheen later in the season, have long petioles and are palmate or pinnately compound. Small creamy-white to pink to reddish-pink flowers are borne in pyramidal clusters well above the foliage in summer, rather like giant astilbes.

Native Habitat Moist woodlands, scrub, and mountainous streamsides in Burma, China, Korea, and Japan

Hardiness Zones USDA 5–8; Sunset 2–9, 14–17, 32–41

Growing Tips Partial shade. Boggy, moist soils and cool temperatures. Mulch in colder zones and protect from drying winter winds.

Cultivars and Related Species *Rodgersia aesculifolia* has palmate leaves that look like those of horse-chestnut and lovely pink flowers. The leaves of *R. pinnata* are bronzy green through most of the growing season, with white ('Superba', 'Alba') or red flowers; *R. podophylla* has wonderful bronze, palmate, pinwheel-shaped leaflets and creamy-white flowers.

Companion Plants Rodgersias offer great background and contrast to all sorts of moisture-loving border companions, including American cranberry bush (*Viburnum opulus* var. *americanum*), Japanese iris (*Iris ensata*), candelabra primroses (*Primula beesiana* and *P. japonica*), and sedges (*Carex*).

Thalictrum | Meadow Rue

Meadow rues are generally tall, with lacy, glaucous compound foliage reminiscent of a giant maidenhair fern. They are superb shady border plants for airy effect and delicate leaf tracery. Sturdy, hollow stems two to five feet tall support compound flower clusters of showy, colorful stamens in white, yellow, pink, lilac-pink, lavender, and violet surrounded by four petallike sepals.

Native Habitat Streams, meadows, and moist, shady mountainous regions worldwide, mainly in northern temperate zone

Hardiness Zones USDA 5–9; Sunset 2–10, 14–17, 32–41

Growing Tips Partial shade. Moist, well-drained, humus-rich soils. Thrives in cool-summer regions. May require support.

Cultivars and Related Species *Thalictrum aquilegiifolium* (columbine meadow rue) is named for its blue-tinted foliage resembling columbine, with lavender flowers in spring atop three-foot-tall stems; *T. flavum* (yellow meadow rue) has divided foliage and thick stems sup-

porting panicles of small yellow flowers in late spring; *T. rochebrunnianum* 'Lavender Mist' is a personal favorite for the back of borders. It is tall and lacy, with dozens of small flowers—lavender-pink sepals enclosing tufts of yellow stamens that dangle from dark purple, four- to six-foot stems.

Companion Plants Grow meadow rues with hydrangeas, Virginia sweetspire (*Itea virginica*), rodgersias, Siberian bugloss (*Brunnera macrophylla*), and hostas.

Tiarella cordifolia | Foamflower

This outstanding native groundcover is indispensable in woodland borders. Foamflowers are clump forming and slowly spread by underground roots and stems to make colonies. Brushlike clusters of tiny, star-shaped white or pink flowers on erect stems to 18 inches tall provide a frothy appearance in spring. The foliage can be heart-shaped or lobed; numerous cultivars offer leaves patterned with darker blotches, centers, and veins. The leaves are evergreen in mild-winter regions.

Native Habitat Woodlands and streambanks in North America and eastern Asia

Hardiness Zones USDA 3–8; Sunset 1–9, 14–24, 32–43

Growing Tips Partial shade. Humus-rich, moderately moist soils with good drainage.

Cultivars and Related Species *Tiarella cordifolia* 'Oakleaf' is a vigorous spreader with dark green, oak-leaf-shaped leaves and pink flower buds and flowers. Hybrid *T.* 'Iron Butterfly' has large fragrant white flowers and striking black-blotched palmately cut foliage edged

Along the margins of a shady woodland border, spring-blooming foamflowers (left) are wonderful partnered with toad lilies, such as 'Miyazaki' (right), which flower for weeks in late summer and fall.

with contrasting green; *T.* 'Brandywine' is superb for its shiny green leaves, creamy-white flowers, and great vigor.

Companion Plants Foamflowers mingle well with small early-blooming spring bulbs like glory-of-the-snow (*Chionodoxa luciliae*), spring starflower (*Ipheion uniflorum*), and grape hyacinths (*Muscari*). They look great with ferns, hostas, creeping phlox (*Phlox stolonifera*), dwarf crested iris (*Iris cristata*), and toad lilies (*Tricyrtis*).

Tricyrtis | Toad Lily

These Asian natives display curious orchidlike blooms for weeks in late summer and fall. The flowers are waxy white to creamy pink and often spotted with purple, ruby red, or maroon. The stems and leaves are often densely hairy. The plants spread by stoloniferous roots but are not considered invasive. Toad lilies are very exotic in appearance and guar-

anteed to inspire comment on autumn border strolls.

Native Habitat Moist woodland, mountains, and cliffs from the eastern Himalaya to the Philippines.

Hardiness Zones USDA 4–8; Sunset 1–9, 14–17, 32–41

Growing Tips Partial shade with late-afternoon sun. Moist, compost-amended soils.

Cultivars and Related Species The leaves of *Tricyrtis formosana* (Formosa toad lily) are softly hairy, with flowers appearing on the upper third of two- to three-foot stems. *T. hirta* (common toad lily) is similar, but the plants are more pendulous than upright, and the late-summer- and fall-blooming maroon- to purple-spotted flowers are set all along the two- to three-foot stems in leaf joints; 'Miyazaki' has white flowers spotted lilac purple. The hybrid *T.* 'Sinonome' offers shiny deep green, spotted foliage and upright-facing white flowers with ruby speckling.

Companion Plants Late-blooming toad lilies harmonize with hybrid anemones (*Anemone × hybrida*), ferns, and sedges (*Carex*) or a simple flat carpet of dark-leafed bugleweed like *Ajuga reptans* 'Chocolate Chip'.

Ornamental Grasses for Shade

Carex | Sedge

Sedges lend variegated and colorful foliage to moist, shady borders. The grasslike leaves sheathing solid, triangular stems may form small tufts or fountains of fine foliage; others are broad-leafed and upright. Foliage colors vary from green to blue, yellow, brown, and orange, plus bold variegations. Flowering is often secondary, although some species have very ornamental inflorescences. Sedge species may be evergreen or deciduous, and they can form clumps or be runners in the border.

Native Habitat Bogs and moist woodlands in temperate regions worldwide

Hardiness Zones USDA 4–9; Sunset 4–9, 14–24, 28–45

Growing Tips Partial shade. Moist, humus-rich soils.

Cultivars and Related Species *Carex siderosticha* 'Variegata', a slow-spreading broad-leafed sedge with green leaves striped with white, can enliven the floor of a shady border. *C. dolichostachya* 'Kaga-nishiki' is a lacy mounded sedge

Its compact size—about ten inches—and eye-catching leaves make *Carex siderosticha* 'Variegata' a popular sedge for edging and filling shady gaps.

with fine gold variegation; it eventually grows to two feet. The palm sedge cultivar *C. muskingumensis* 'Oehme' has gorgeous two-foot green leaves sporting narrow yellow margins that become more evident as the season progresses. It is capable of forming large groundcover masses.

Companion Plants Sedges combine nicely with hostas and coral bells (*Heuchera*), as well as moisture-loving primroses (*Primula*) and ligularias.

Fargesia nitida | Fountain Bamboo

Do not fear—fountain bamboo is modest in size and a slow clump former that will not run rampant through a mixed border. It offers finely textured green foliage and exceptional hardiness. Upright in form, the polished dark mahogany to purple-black stems (culms) grow slowly to 12 feet high. Its leaves are lance-shaped and a glaucous gray-green. New stems remain unbranched during their first year of growth and sprout very

few leaves—don't mistake these for dead stems.

Native Habitat Streams and damp woodlands in central China

Hardiness Zones USDA 4–10; Sunset 3–24, 29–41

Growing Tips Partial or light, dappled shade; also grows in full sun. Fertile, moisture-retentive soils. Shelter from cold, drying winter winds.

Cultivars and Related Species *Fargesia murielae* is very similar but grows with lax, arching stems.

Companion Plants Fountain bamboo makes a nice background for a shady mixed border; single specimens provide elegant vertical focal points. Mix it with oakleaf hydrangea (*Hydrangea quercifolia*), fothergilla (*Fothergilla gardenii*), Solomon's seals (*Polygonatum*), coral bells (*Heuchera*), or the dark-leafed white snakeroot *Eupatorium rugosum* 'Chocolate'.

Hakonechloa macra 'Aureola'
'Aureola' Hakone Grass

Exquisite grace and beauty are apt descriptions of Hakone grass. This low-mounding perennial grass has cascades of arching, linear foliage to two feet long. The leaves of 'Aureola' are a bright yellow-chartreuse with narrow stripes of green that may become red-flushed in autumn. In late summer to mid-autumn, open clusters of pale green spikelets (flowers) appear above the foliage.

Native Habitat Garden cultivar; species: wooded, mountainous areas of Japan

Hardiness Zones USDA 5–9; Sunset 2–9, 14–24, 31–41

Growing Tips Partial shade for best leaf color. Fertile, humus-rich, moist but well-drained soils.

Cultivars and Related Species *Hakonechloa macra* 'All Gold' has more upright leaves than 'Aureola' and a glowing solid golden-yellow color. 'Albo-striata' offers white-striped leaves.

Companion Plants Accent Hakone grass against dark-leafed bugbanes (*Actaea simplex* 'Brunette'), blue-leafed hostas such as *Hosta* 'Blue Angel' or 'Halcyon', or a flat, dark-leafed bugleweed like *Ajuga reptans* 'Chocolate Chip'.

Milium effusum 'Aureum'
Bowles' Golden Grass

A clumping plant to two feet high, Bowles' golden grass has an erect habit at first and then arches as its leaves expand. Nodding clusters of tiny golden spikelets bloom above the rich yellow foliage in late spring to early summer. Spring and partial shade bring out the best in this grass, which tends to fizzle in hot summer weather.

Native Habitat Garden hybrid; species: woodlands in temperate regions of eastern North America, Europe, and Asia

Hardiness Zones USDA 5–9; Sunset 3–9; 14–17, 31–34, 39

Growing Tips Light shade. Humus-rich, moist but well-drained soils. Cut back in early summer to encourage new growth.

Cultivars and Related Species None

Companion Plants This golden grass is stellar with the dark-splotched foliage of the cranesbill *Geranium phaeum* 'Samobor' or the variegated Siberian bugloss *Brunnera macrophylla* 'Hadspen Cream'. It also is sensational poking through clumps of purple-leafed coral

Fallen magnolia petals on a stand of kuma bamboo grass bring out the buff tones of the leaf edges.

bells such as *Heuchera* 'Purple Petticoats' or 'Plum Pudding' or *Ligularia dentata* 'Desdemona.'

Sasa veitchii | Kuma Bamboo Grass

Kuma bamboo grass is a moderate to vigorous spreader, but its beauty warrants the effort it takes to control it. It has coarse, dark green, lance-shaped ribbed leaves that turn whitish buff all around the edges for a variegated effect in fall and winter. The plant reaches three to four feet tall after several years.

Native Habitat Damp hollows and woodlands in Japan

Hardiness Zones USDA 6–10; Sunset 4–24, 29–41

Growing Tips Light to dense shade. Sandy or clay soils with regular moisture. To control spread, use a sharp digging spade or edging tool to cut off errant rhizomes and emerging shoots or install root barriers.

Cultivars and Related Species *Sasa palmata* grows to five feet tall, with broad, handsome leaves that spread fingerlike from stems and branch tips.

Companion Plants Kuma bamboo grass is often mass-planted in Japanese-style gardens: Try it with hydrangeas such as *Hydrangea paniculata* 'Kyushu', the Japanese anemone (*Anemone* × *hybrida*) 'Honorine Jobert', or the toad lily *Tricyrtis* 'Sinonome'.

Annuals for Shade

In most regions, the following plants are treated as annuals, but some may be perennial in frost-free areas.

Begonia Semperflorens Cultorum Group | Wax Begonia, Semperflorens Begonia

Gardeners are most familiar with semperflorens begonias—a group of fibrous-rooted begonias that are bedded out and grown as annuals in most regions. They are bushy and compact, up to a foot tall, with juicy stems that produce lots of small flowers from spring through fall. The waxy foliage can be green, red, bronze, or variegated. Sometimes considered a bit pedestrian, waxleaf begonias can add artful touches of flower and foliage color to mixed shade borders.

Native Habitat Varied habitat in tropical and subtropical regions worldwide

Growing Tips Partial shade to brighter exposures out of direct sun. Well-drained, humus-rich, neutral to slightly acidic soils.

Cultivars and Related Species Underused *Begonia fuchsioides* (fuchsia begonia) is really worth a try. It is shrublike, to 30 inches tall, with small, shiny, sickle-shaped leaves and fuchsia-like pink to red flowers. From a distance it masquerades as a fuchsia but holds up much bet-

ter in hot summer regions. *B. grandis* subsp. *evansiana* (hardy begonia) is a true perennial in USDA Zones 6–9; Sunset 3–33. It is upright with notched olive-green leaves and hanging clusters of fragrant pink or white flowers.

Companion Plants Waxleaf begonias make interesting bedfellows with the golden sedge *Carex dolichostachya* 'Kaga-nishiki', ferns, hostas, bleeding hearts (*Dicentra*), and Siberian bugloss (*Brunnera macrophylla*).

Fuchsia | Fuchsia

Fuchsias always attract attention because of their unusual pendant, tubular flowers, which are often bicolored, with the corolla (inside part of the flower) one hue and the outside tube and four sepals either white, red, or pinkish to purple. Single flowers have four petals and exquisite form; doubles and full doubles sport eight or more petals and can resemble puffy ball gowns. Hummingbirds love to drink nectar from fuchsia flowers.

Native Habitat Mountainous areas of Central and South America and New Zealand

Growing Tips Partial shade best but can take morning sun. Does not tolerate high summer heat or humidity. Fertile, moist, well-drained soils. Control fuchsia gall mites (a serious problem in California) by cutting off and destroying affected leaves or selecting mite-resistent species and cultivars.

Cultivars and Related Species *Fuchsia magellanica* is an arching shrub with three-foot stems loaded with drooping small flowers with red tubes and violet-purple corollas. It is the hardiest fuchsia

The hardy begonia's lush, red-tinged leaves and clusters of pink or white flowers from midsummer on add a tropical tone to the shady border.

Far from jarring, deep pink impatiens enhance the subtle hues of Japanese painted fern and wishbone flower.

(USDA Zones 6–9; Sunset 3–9, 14–24, 31–32, with lots of winter protection in colder zones). *F.* 'Gartenmeister Bonstedt' is a vigorous two-foot-tall heat-tolerant fuchsia with dark bronze-red leaves with purple undersides and very long-tubed, brick-red flowers; 'Traudchen Bonstedt', with green foliage and pale pink tubular flowers, shares the same qualities. Finer-textured *F. thymifolia* is erect and spreading, with small leaves and a profusion of tiny dangling white to pink-red flowers.

Companion Plants Fuchsias combine effectively with colorful foliage plants like coleus (*Solenostemon scutellarioides*), dark-leafed taros like *Colocasia* 'Black Magic' and *C.* 'Illustris', hostas, and sedges (*Carex*).

Impatiens | Impatiens

With more than 850 species and several cultivated series comprising scores of varieties, impatiens are among the most popular shade annuals for mixed borders. They provide long-lasting summer color—breeding has become so sophisticated that you can select just the right hue for your border. The asymetrical five-petaled flowers, borne in clusters, are often spurred and sometimes hooded (depending on species). They are followed by explosive seed capsules that will burst open at a touch. In warmer areas, deadhead to limit reseeding.

Native Habitat Damp areas near streams or lakes or in woodlands throughout tropical and warm-temperate regions (except Australia, New Zealand, and South America)

Growing Tips Partial shade. Humus-rich, moist but well-drained soil. Shelter from wind.

Cultivars and Related Species *Impatiens walleriana* possesses light green to red-flushed stems. Depending on the cultivated series, they can reach 18 inches in height and produce flattened, slender-spurred flowers in white and numerous shades of orange, yellow, pink, red, violet, purple, and lavender-blue, plus bicolors.

Companion Plants Impatiens partner harmoniously with just about any shade perennial or shrub. Combine them with ferns, coral bells (*Heuchera*), kirengeshomas, or coleus (*Solenostemon scutellarioides*).

Solenostemon scutellarioides Coleus

From the windowsill to the mixed border, the coleus revolution continues to thrive. Grown as annuals or short-lived perennials for their wildly colorful foliage, coleus plants have succulent, square stems bearing leaves in a variety of shapes from rounded to frilly and lobed; most are coarsely toothed. Colors span the spectrum, with the exception of blue. Throughout the year

they produce racemelike whorls of tiny, tubular, two-lipped blue, white, or purple flowers.

Native Habitat Forests in tropical Africa and Asia

Growing Tips Partial shade or full sun. Humus-rich, moist but well-drained soil with lots of organic matter. Water freely in dry weather. Pinch to produce bushy plants, and deadhead flowers to keep plants vigorous.

Cultivars and Related Species
Solenostemon scutellarioides 'India Frills' is a diminutive coleus with a spreading, compact habit and one-inch, irregularly lobed leaves of green, red, and bright yellow; 'Japanese Giant' boasts large leaves of vivid green rimmed and veined in maroon; 'Sedona' struts leaves in magnificent sunset shades of orange and gold, with hints of red. *S.* 'Kiwi Fern' sports fern-shaped leaves of burgundy with light cream, slightly ruffled edging.

Companion Plants Bed coleus against shrubs like the golden-leafed elderberry *Sambucus racemosa* 'Sutherland Gold', or partner it with ferns, spiderworts (*Tradescantia*), Siberian bugloss (*Brunnera macrophylla*), meadow rues (*Thalictrum*), or hostas.

Torenia fournieri | Wishbone Flower
Wishbone flowers are grown for their short clusters of tubular flowers with flared, two-lipped mouths. In summer, this species produces abundant lilac-blue flowers to 1½ inches long, the lower lips deep purple and the throats marked yellow. Several color series have been developed offering flowers in white, pink, deep purple, or lavender blue.

Wildly variable in color, size, and leaf shape, coleus holds its own grown in masses or harmonizing with other plants, such as begonias.

Plant wishbone flower near the border's edge to get the most of its interesting-looking, cool-toned blooms.

Native Habitat High altitude woodlands in tropical Asia

Growing Tips Partial shade. Fertile, moist but well-drained soil. Does not like extreme heat and humidity.

Cultivars and Related Species Cultivars in the *Torenia fournieri* Clown series produce compact plants with white, pink, deep purple, or lavender flowers and better heat tolerance than the species.

Companion Plants Plantings of wishbone flowers enhance ferns, hostas, sedges (*Carex*), and coral bells, particularly *Heuchera americana* 'Dale's Strain'.

Bulbs for Shade

Caladium bicolor
Caladium, Angel Wings

Caladiums are luminous foliage plants rising from underground tubers. They bear odd greenish-white spathes (leaflike bracts enclosing a flower cluster, or spadix), but their real appeal is in the foliage. Leaves come in solid pastels to deep greens and reds and are often splashed, streaked, spotted, or edged with contrasting colors. The peltate leaves vary from roundish to arrow- or lance-shaped and are held high on slender petioles.

Native Habitat Woodland margins in tropical South America

Hardiness Zones USDA 9–11; Sunset 12, 13, 16, 17, 22–27

Growing Tips Partial to full shade. Moist, well-drained, humus-rich, slightly acidic soils. Dig tubers in fall in regions where not winter-hardy and store in a cool, dry place.

Cultivars and Related Species *Caladium bicolor* 'Gingerland' is a beauty, with 6-

to 12-inch, strap-shaped gray-green leaves with white ribs, dark green edges, and maroon spots; *C.* 'June Bride' lightens up borders with silvery-white leaves with green veins. My favorite is 'Kathleen', which shines with 8- to 16-inch green-edged pink leaves.

Companion Plants Caladiums lend a tropical edge to the border and make an interesting textural mix with other bold-leafed shrubs and perennials like variegated Japanese angelica tree (*Aralia elata* 'Variegata'), *Astilboides tabularis*, Korean angelica (*Angelica gigas*), hostas, geraniums, and astilbes.

Colocasia esculenta | Taro
The large, wavy-edged, heart- to arrow-shaped leaves of taros add big, bold, tropical flair to the shady border. Originating from underground tubers, the leaves are mostly dark green, often with prominent contrasting veins. They reach two to three feet long on slender leaf stems.

Native Habitat Swampy or moist areas of tropical eastern Asia

Hardiness Zones USDA Zones 9–11; Sunset 12, 16–28

Growing Tips Partial shade. Fertile, humus-rich, moist soils. Tolerates wet soils and often grown as marginal aquatic plant. Dig and store tubers or overwinter in containers in cool, dry location.

Cultivars and Related Species *Colocasia esculenta* 'Black Magic' is the taro of the moment, with leaves that often start green but soon turn a luscious dark purplish black with a glaucous sheen; 'Illustris' sports green leaves with a dark gray to black overlay, white veining, and edges of lime green.

Companion Plants Taros make effective accent or specimen plants. Mix them with fountain bamboo (*Fargesia nitida*), sedges (*Carex*), caladiums, cranesbills (*Geranium*), or with an underplanting of coral bells (*Heuchera*). Use them as a dark background for *Dahlia* 'Bishop of Llandaff.'

Hedychium | Ginger Lily
Ginger lilies are prized for their late-summer and early-fall floral display atop tall, bold-foliaged stalks. Their intoxicating fragrance is reminiscent of a very sweet honeysuckle. They have thick, fleshy rhizomes and usually lance-shaped leaves borne in two parallel ranks on unbranched reedlike stems.

Native Habitat Moist, lightly wooded areas of Asia (particularly northern India and the Himalaya)

Hardiness Zones USDA 7–10; Sunset 16, 17, 22–27

Taros, especially multicolored cultivars like 'Illustris', make striking focal points in moist, shady gardens.

Kahili ginger's frilly, red-stamened flowers stand tall and bold in late summer.

Growing Tips Partial shade or sun. Humus-rich, moist, well-drained soils. Grow against a warm wall and provide deep winter mulch where marginally hardy (USDA 7–8; Sunset 16–17), or dig and store in cool, dry location.

Cultivars and Related Species Hybrid *Hedychium* 'Elizabeth' is tall and imposing, topping out at ten feet with clusters of giant, brilliant reddish-orange flowers. *H. coronarium* (white ginger) has butterfly-like white flowers on five- to six-foot-tall stems and is very fragrant; *H. gardnerianum* (Kahili ginger) forms upright six- to seven-foot-tall clumps with lance-shaped grayish-green leaves and aromatic lemon-yellow flowers with bright red stamens. Several *Hedychium* species are considered invasive in Hawaii and have been found growing wild in several southern states. In climates where *Hedychium* is hardy, remove the flower heads before they form seeds and pull up spreading shoots.

Companion Plants Combine ginger lilies with cannas, coleus (*Solenostemon scutellarioides*), toad lilies (*Tricyrtis*), *Astilboides tabularis*, or taros (*Colocasia*) and elephant's ear (*Alocasia*).

Xanthosoma violaceum | Blue Taro
This foliage plant par excellence has thick-stemmed, arrow-shaped leaves that grow to 24 inches long and 18 inches wide. The foliage is powdery dark green above, lighter beneath, with purplish veins and margins and dark purple stems with a heavy, waxy blue or gray cast. The inflorescence (which is secondary in attraction to the foliage) is a yellowish-white spathe surrounding a white spadix.

Native Habitat Tropical U.S., Central and South America

Hardiness Zones USDA 9–11; Sunset 17, 22–24

Growing Tips Partial shade. Slightly acidic, humus-rich, well-drained soils. Fertilize frequently in active growth. Dig and store tubers or overwinter in containers in cool, dry location.

Cultivars and Related Species *Xanthosoma sagittifolium* 'Lime Zinger' and 'Chartreuse Giant' offer beautiful bright lime-green to chartreuse leaves that electify shady borders.

Companion Plants Blue taro partners well with coleus (*Solenostemon scutellarioides*), gingers (*Hedychium*), spiderworts (*Tradescantia*), and caladiums.

Zantedeschia aethiopica
Common Calla Lily
Common calla lily forms hefty clumps of long-stalked, shiny rich green, arrow-

Golden calla glows in the shady border, with 'Walter Turner' coleus adding to the play of light and dark.

shaped leaves 18 inches long and 10 inches wide. From late spring to mid-summer, a succession of large, pure white or cream-colored spathes appear on three-foot stems surrounding a creamy-yellow central spike (spadix) composed of tiny true flowers.

Native Habitat Moist soils, swamps, or lake margins in southern and eastern Africa.

Hardiness Zones USDA 8–10; Sunset 5, 6, 8, 9, 12–29

Growing Tips Partial shade or full sun. Humus-rich, moist soils. Can be grown as a marginal aquatic plant. Over-winter indoors in containers in cool, dry location.

Cultivars and Related Species
Zantedeschia aethiopica 'Green Goddess' is a robust cultivar with large spathes that are white at the base and green at the tips. *Z. elliottiana* (golden calla)

yields heart-shaped, dark green basal foliage covered with translucent white spots. Golden-yellow spathes surround spadices of the same hue. Other flower colors have been hybridized for the cut-flower trade and are now available for garden use.

Companion Plants Calla lilies may be considered pedestrian in some regions, but to most gardeners they are exotic and worth a try. Combine them with ferns, coleus (*Solenostemon scutellarioides*), *Darmera peltata*, Japanese iris (*Iris ensata*), ligularias, and rodgersias.

From Plan to Planting: Tips for Installing Your Border

Prepare the Planting Bed

Once you are happy with your garden plan and have determined the size and placement of your border, it's time to prepare the planting bed. If the area is currently covered in turf, the first step is to get rid of the grass. One earth-friendly method is to cover the entire bed with black, six-millimeter polyethylene sheeting, securely pegged down with stakes, stones, or wooden planks to keep it in place. Heat generated by the sun and retained by the plastic will burn off grass and weeds, usually within several months. At the end of the process, remove the plastic, roll or fold it up, and store it for future use. Then amend the solarized soil with one part compost or well-rotted manure for every two parts soil. The easiest way to determine how much compost to add is to take a standard digging shovel and sink it into the soil. If the entire shovel blade sinks fairly easily into the bed with foot pressure, you have approximately one foot of soil, and you need to add about four inches of compost. If the shovel goes only eight inches deep, work in two to three inches of compost.

I prefer the less labor-intensive, no-till method of covering the bed with 12 to 16 sheets of newspaper, which is biodegradable, and topping it with three to four inches of compost. Put down the paper in several layers with generous overlapping seams and thoroughly cover it with compost. Moisten it well and allow the bed to sit undisturbed for several weeks while the grass and weeds below the paper and mulch are smothered. When you're ready to plant, you can simply dig holes right through the compost and the gradually decomposing paper.

Calculate Plant Quantities and Spacing

The most common mistake made when creating a border is placing plants too close together. After a growing season or so, they become entangled and fail to get adequate light or air circulation, which often results in weakened or diseased plants. In a perfectly planted, mature border, full, rounded crowns of foliage slightly overlap each other, leaving no blank spaces for weeds to grow.

The best way to determine the optimal spacing for plants—and how many plants to buy—is to know their mature height and spread. The "Encyclopedia of Plants for Sun and Shade" (page 28) provides this information for a variety of mixed-border plants. Garden-plant reference books, horticulture websites, and the tags on nursery-bought plants are also helpful guides. Use this information to estimate the number of plants you'll need for a particular spot—spacing is not an exact science that requires you to get down on the ground with a tape measure. In general, I like to space small, low-growing annuals, perennials, and groundcovers 6 to 8 inches apart; midsize and larger perennials 12 to 18 inches apart; and shrubs 3 to 6 feet apart.

Shop for Plants

A full-service garden center, specialty nursery, or mail-order nursery will offer shrubs, perennials, and annuals grown in easy-to-carry containers in a variety of sizes and prices to fit your budget. Larger specimen shrubs for mixed borders that will provide an instant framework for your border may be balled and burlapped, meaning they've been dug to preserve the entire rootball, which is wrapped in protective fabric. At the appropriate planting times, garden centers feature a selection of dormant bulbs for spring or summer bloom; mail-order sources send out catalogs months before. A word of caution: Don't go hog-wild buying plants the first year. Keep your plan in mind and go slow. You can always add more plants later.

Unpack the plants as soon as they arrive or when you get them home from the nursery. Keep them in a cool, shaded area until you can get them into the ground. Water containerized plants well. If plants are shipped bare-root, unpack them immediately and inspect the roots for signs of damage. Cut off any broken, damaged, or rotting portions. If the roots are dry, soak them in warm water for several hours prior to planting; if you're not putting them into the border right away, pot them up.

Lay Out the Planting

Rake the bed surface smooth. Using your plan as a guide, lay out your plants on top of the soil. If you acquire all the plants beforehand, you can lay out the entire border before you plant. When I see actual plant combinations in place, I often change my mind and make alterations on the spot. It's also easy to make spacing adjustments after the border is laid out. Measure the length of your hand trowel or shovel handle for quick reference in plant spacing.

Plant the Border

Installing containerized plants is easy, but here are a few tips that will lead to greater success. To remove the plant from its container, cup your hand around the plant's crown and invert the pot. Gently shake the container or rap the rim on a solid surface to dislodge the plant. Refrain from pulling the plant out of the container by its stems or leaves, which may damage the plant or break it from its roots.

If the plant is pot-bound, use your fingers or a clawed weeding tool to comb out any tight, circling, or badly bent and twisted roots and cut them off with sharp, clean pruners. Be brutal—the best thing you can do for a container-grown plant prior to planting is to loosen up the roots.

Dig a hole twice as wide and three to five inches deeper than the longest roots. Make a cone of soil in the center of the hole. It should be tall enough to bring the crown of the plant level with the soil surface. Spread the roots evenly over the mound. Holding the crown in place, fill the hole with soil. Firm the soil around the crown, level it to grade, and water the plant well. Never let the soil around a new plant dry out during the first growing season.

Installing a bare-root plant is easy because you don't have to break up the root ball as you do with containerized stock. Dig a hole in a well-prepared bed and plant as above.

Water the Border

During the first year, watering is crucial to allow new plants to get established. Even drought-tolerant plants adapted to dry climates require adequate watering during their first growing season.

Use soaker hoses or drip irrigation to get water into the soil and to the roots with minimal loss to evaporation. After planting, loop soaker hoses through the border, spacing the loops around plants according to the manufacturer's suggestions. After the hoses are in place, cover them with a camouflage of water-conserving mulch. On average, moist- and wet-soil borders require an inch of water per week. Plants adapted to dry conditions can get by with less. If rainfall is insufficient, turn on soaker hoses manually or connect them to timers that will turn on and shut off the system automatically. The manufacturer's directions will tell you how long it takes the system to deliver the equivalent of one inch of rain.

Fertilize the Border

The best way to fertilize is to build up the soil with well-composted manure and other organic matter over time. Top-dress borders with compost, mulch, or shredded leaves at least once during the growing season to continually build humus-rich, moisture-retentive organic soil. I like to broadcast a granular organic fertilizer around annuals when I plant them.

Mulch the Border

The best way to conserve soil moisture, help suppress weeds, and keep borders looking tidy is to cover them with a one- to two-inch layer of mulch early in the growing season before new growth starts. Think regionally when you choose mulch—local materials blend more naturally in the garden and are less expensive because they are produced nearby, and buying them supports the local economy. I prefer organic mulches like chopped leaves, well-composted manure, or fine to medium-grade shredded bark. Organic mulches insulate the soil and at the same time slowly release nitrogen and other nutrients for good plant growth. Manure from horses, sheep, and cows is good, but not fresh from the barn or stables—it needs to be aged so it doesn't burn the plants. Manure is usually mixed with some kind of bedding, such as sawdust, wood chips, or straw. Shredding the manure grinds up and blends in the bedding, making a fine- to medium-textured mulch that is attractive and easy to apply. Rock and gravel mulches are appropriate in some regions, particularly the arid West. Fine-textured rock from local sources blends seamlessly with the native stone so prominent in these regions and is a great soil insulator.

Prevent Pests and Diseases

One of the most important things you can do to keep pests and diseases at bay is to choose plants wisely at the outset, making sure to pick species and cultivars that are suited to the growing conditions and climate in your area. Select plant varieties that have been bred for better resistance to mildew, rusts, and other foliage diseases. If you match the plants to the site, install them properly, and give them the care they need—frequent application of compost, proper and timely pruning, wise watering, and good sanitation—you'll have few problems.

Learn to live with minor insect damage. When the border is in balance, beneficial predatory insects and insect-eating animals, such as birds and bats, keep most pests in check. If a bug gets out of control or there is a disease outbreak, refer to reliable references such as Brooklyn Botanic garden handbooks *Natural Insect Control* and *Natural Disease Control* for least-toxic treatment strategies.

Stake Plants as Necessary

Tall perennials and annuals have a tendency to flop, particularly when laden with flowers or exposed to strong winds and rain. Humus-rich, loamy soils, as well as over-fertilization during the growing season, promote fast, succulent growth that falls over easily. Keeping plants on a leaner diet may help produce sturdier stems, but staking is sometimes inevitable.

In mixed borders, you can often take advantage of close-growing shrubs and sturdy, strong-stemmed perennials like summer phlox, Joe-pye weeds (*Eupatorium*), and coneflowers (*Echinacea* and *Rudbeckia*), to help support flop-prone plants. Tall, narrow flower spikes like those of delphiniums, lilies, and blazing stars (*Liatris*) can be individually tied to slender stakes stuck in the ground alongside the stems. Full-crowned plants like peonies are best grown through wire hoops, placed over the emerging clumps in spring. The hoops will disappear as the foliage and flowers engulf them. Another technique is to insert five bamboo stakes in the ground around the perimeter of the clump and then tie twine to the stakes in a star pattern, crisscrossing between the emerging stems for support. My favorite method of supporting border plants is pea-staking—using two- to four-foot multibranched shrub or tree prunings poked in and around the emerging crowns and foliage of leafy perennials. The foliage grows up and around these natural twiggy supports, rendering them invisible.

Index and Contributors

Contributors

Bob Hyland is co-owner and manager of Loomis Creek Nursery, a retail nursery in New York's Hudson River Valley that specializes in perennials, grasses, shrubs, and tender plants for mixed borders. He is former vice-president of horticulture and operations at Brooklyn Botanic Garden. His peripatetic career at Strybing Arboretum and Botanical Gardens in San Francisco and Longwood Gardens in Pennsylvania has acquainted him with plants from around the world.

Illustrations

Steve Buchanan

Photos

Saxon Holt cover and page 7 (entry garden at San Francisco Botanical Garden)

Rob Cardillo pages 2, 32 both, 42, 44, 46, 48, 49, 53, 57, 59, 67, 71, 72, 73, 74 left, 81, 83, 104, 105, 108

David Cavagnaro pages 4, 8, 12, 25, 31, 39, 40, 50, 52, 55, 65, 68, 69, 70, 75, 76, 77, 84, 88, 90, 91, 96, 100 left, 103, 109, 110

New England Wild Flower Society page 6 (display gardens at nursery)

Bob Hyland pages 11, 23

Alan & Linda Detrick pages 14, 26, 34 left, 36, 45 (and back cover), 74 right, 82, 87, 92, 97, 100 right

Jerry Pavia pages 28 (Coglizer garden designed by Freeland & Sabrina Tanner), 33, 34 right, 35, 37 both, 41, 43, 47, 51, 58, 63, 64, 66, 79, 94, 101, 106

Derek Fell pages 30, 80, 89, 95

Charles Mann pages 54 (and back cover), 56 (and back cover), 60, 62, 93

Netherlands Flower Bulb Info Center page 78

Christine Douglas pages 86, 98, 107

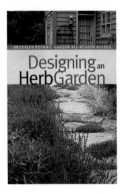

More Information on Designing Dazzling Borders

Designing an Herb Garden has everything you need to create a dazzling garden that's ornamental, practical, and fragrant, including simple plans, plant recommendations for each design, lushly photographed herb profiles, and indispensable cultivation advice.

In *Annuals for Every Garden,* you'll find the plants that are just right for designing a spectacular ever-changing annual border, a display of drought-resistant flowers, an evening garden, and more, along with seed-starting and growing tips.

Ordering Books From Brooklyn Botanic Garden

World renowned for pioneering gardening information, Brooklyn Botanic Garden's award-winning guides provide practical advice for gardeners in every region of North America.

Join Brooklyn Botanic Garden as an annual Subscriber Member and receive three gardening handbooks, delivered directly to you, each year. Other benefits include free admission to many public gardens across the country, plus three issues of *Plants & Gardens News, Members News,* and our guide to courses and public programs.

For additional information about Brooklyn Botanic Garden, including other membership packages, call 718-623-7210 or visit our website at www.bbg.org. To order other fine titles published by BBG, call 718-623-7286 or shop in our online store at www.bbg.org/gardengiftshop.